The
Mediterranean
Diet Weight Loss
Solution

The
Mediterranean Diet Weight Loss
Solution

The 28-Day Kick-Start Plan for Lasting Weight Loss

JULENE STASSOU, MS, RD

Foreword by
Mark S. Sapienza, MD

ROCKRIDGE
PRESS

For general information on our other products and services or to obtain technical support, please contact our Customer Care Department within the United States at (866) 744-2665, or outside the United States at (510) 253-0500.

Photography © Grinvalds/Shutterstock.com, cover; Africa Studio/Shutterstock.com, cover; Rua Castilho/ Stockfood, cover; Foxes Forest Manufacture/ Shutterstock.com, cover & p. ii; Dobranska Renata/ Stocksy, p. vi; Arts Illustrated Studios/Shutterstock. com, p. ix; Darren Muir/Stocksy, p. x; Duet Postscriptum/Stocksy, pp. xiv & 1; Image4stock/ Shutterstock.com, p. 2; Irina Vaneeva/Shutterstock. com, p. 7 (background); Mountain Brothers/ Shutterstock.com, p. 7 (food); Bisual Studio/Stocksy, p. 8; Evi Abeler (photos) & Albane Sharrard (food styling), pp. 10, 70, 98, 150, 162, 180 & 194; Micky Wiswedel/Stocksy, p. 26; Inspiring/Shutterstock. com, pp. 33-36; Milles Studio/Stocksy, pp. 40 & 41; Fortyforks/Shutterstock.com, p. 42; Ostap Senyuk/ Unsplash.com, pp. 82 & 83; People Pictures/Stockfood, pp. 84, 122 & back cover; White Ramekins/Stockfood, p. 108; Mario Matassa/Stockfood, p. 138 & back cover.

Author photo © Chris Marksbury

ISBN: Print 978-1-62315-940-5
eBook: 978-1-62315-941-2

R2

This book is dedicated to my wonderful children, Ella Juliet and Jake Theodore, and to my mother, Rhea, and yiayia, Julia, for teaching me how to cook and making everything taste so good.

Contents

◇◇◇◇◇◇◇◇◇◇◇◇◇◇◇◇◇◇◇◇◇◇◇◇◇◇

Foreword   viii
Introduction   xi

PART 1   GETTING STARTED

1 Your Mediterranean Diet Primer   3

2 Tackling Weight Loss   11

3 Exercise, Rest, *and* Relaxation   27

PART 2   YOUR 28-DAY COMMITMENT

4 The 28-Day Plan   43

5 Beyond 28 Days   71

PART 3   THE RECIPES

6 Breakfast   85

7 Snacks   99

8 Salads *and* Soups   109

9 Starches *and* Grains   123

10 Beans, Legumes, *and* Vegetable Mains   139

11 Fish *and* Seafood   151

12 Poultry *and* Meat   163

13 Easy Vegetable Sides   181

14 Sweets   195

Measurement Conversions 204
The Dirty Dozen *and* the Clean Fifteen 205
Resources 206

References 207
Recipe Index 210
Index 212

Foreword

◇◇◇◇◇◇◇◇◇◇◇◇◇◇◇◇◇◇◇◇◇◇◇◇◇◇◇◇◇◇◇◇◇◇

Working as a gastroenterologist in a busy private practice in Bergen County, New Jersey, I encounter many different ailments and afflictions associated with this specialty of medicine. Whether treating ulcers and heartburn or performing a colonoscopy to screen for cancer, we in this field are accustomed to treating a wide array of intestinal disorders. Among the more common challenges we face on a daily basis are obesity and ensuring our patients have a good diet and proper nutrition. This is not an easy task for a doctor when patient-doctor time is already limited and there are numerous medical factors that influence nutrition and a plethora of diet plans to consider. As physicians, we often fall short in educating our patients on the merits of a good diet and why they should lose weight. We simply don't have the time or the resources.

So we, as a medical practice, turned to Julene Stassou—a registered dietitian with a master's degree in nutrition education. For the past few years she has been working with some of our patients and setting them on the correct path. She doesn't do this simply by handing them a piece of paper with a diet and dismissing them. Instead, she sits down with them, educates them, and formulates a diet plan tailored to each patient's needs. In essence, she becomes their nutritional coach. With *The Mediterranean Diet Weight Loss Solution*, Julene has synthesized this approach into a simple yet actionable plan that so many of us, swept up in the chaos of everyday life, can on our own put to good use to lose weight and improve health. Unlike so many of today's fad diets, which are impractical in the long term and often unpleasant to endure

in the short term, the Mediterranean diet that Julene brings you is not only easy to replicate and enjoyable to the palate, but also clearly and statistically associated with cardiovascular and medical benefits.

The Mediterranean diet is more than just a diet—it's a sustainable way of life. I saw this and experienced it even as a youth spending summers in Sicily with my family on the slopes of Mount Etna. I've seen firsthand the positive effect this diet has on health and how it can help people thrive. We can't bring everyone to live in Italy or Greece, but Julene has found a way to bring that lifestyle to you in the comfort of your own home.

Mark S. Sapienza, MD
Chief of Gastroenterology at Englewood Hospital in New Jersey

Introduction

I believe what we put into our bodies can serve as a primary determinant of how we function, feel, and look. Whether you "eat to live" or "live to eat," you can nurture your body through food choices. Food isn't just fuel; it's a means by which we can maintain our overall health and well-being. The countless vitamins and minerals in foods each have a purpose—they facilitate efficient operation of our body.

As a registered dietitian, my primary role is that of a health care provider, but I also bring a culinary background and passion. This passion goes beyond wanting to be healthy. It is a deep desire to help people reach their goals. It brings me tremendous joy and satisfaction to see my patients succeed in whatever it is they came to me to achieve. I love this field and how I can make a difference for people—and perhaps this love affair came from my upbringing.

Growing up in a large Greek family, I learned that everything centered on food. The smell of baking bread constantly filled the air. Our pantry staples included fresh fruits and vegetables, and olive oil—lots of it. As a child, I would get up early on Saturdays to cook my family breakfast, help my mother and *yiayia* (the Greek word for grandmother) cook traditional foods, and strive to make the perfect baklava. When I went off to college, it made total sense to major in food and restaurant management. I got a full-time job in hospital food service, an experience that quickly signaled to me that meals are not always prepared in the healthiest manner. The sodium, fat, and calorie counts were sorely excessive. With obesity levels in the country rising by epic proportions, and heart disease becoming the leading killer among Americans, I was alarmed. I knew I wanted to do more—to use my knowledge of food to help people get *healthy*. So I returned to school for dietetics, got my master's of science in nutrition education from Columbia University, and became clinically trained in all areas of food and healthy eating.

Almost 20 years later, my passion continues. I have a private practice devoted to helping people lose weight, keep it off, and maintain healthy lifestyles. I provide therapeutic diets for people facing various diseases and maladies. They are living with high cholesterol, high blood pressure, and diabetes, to name a few of their issues. Most of my patients come to me after struggling to lose weight without success. Their stories are moving: They have tried every diet on the market. They are downtrodden from counting points, spending money they don't have on shakes and supplements, and feeling heavier and sicker than ever. They are justifiably angry, sad, and frustrated. We talk, and we formulate a plan. This plan is not a diet in the way we think of diets; rather, it's a strategy for moving forward with a different mind-set—a plan for life.

After just a few days of eating better, my patients are calling me. Yes, they are losing weight. But they have been transformed in ways that surprise them—they feel energized, they're sleeping better, and they are happier. Best of all, they are, for the first time, hopeful. People who "couldn't lose a pound" were back in my office with tears of joy and messages of self-empowerment. Through education and guidance, they were able to break through the barriers that hold people back and find the way to enduring weight loss and optimum health.

If you have tried without success to lose weight, it's understandable you could feel daunted, even pessimistic, about the prospect. The Mediterranean diet is a common-sense approach to food that avoids hype, fads, and processed "weight-loss" novelties. We will explore the science behind the success of this diet. We'll discuss the importance of exercise, rest, relaxation, and mindfulness as they pertain to weight loss. And we'll illustrate the benefits of this diet beyond weight loss, including disease prevention.

Perhaps one of the less-touted reasons for its success is that the Mediterranean diet still provides the opportunity for people to "eat, drink, and be merry." You will not be drinking a canned shake or choking down a tasteless bar—quite the opposite. This is palate-pleasing, dinner-party-worthy fare that feels good and sticks to the ribs.

Research shows that the Mediterranean diet is one of the most successful diets out there in a sea of options, and you will soon see for yourself that this is truly a delicious, realistic, and sustainable method—both to lose weight and to maintain a healthy weight.

This book provides an actionable, easy-to-follow 28-day program to kick-start weight loss and put you on the path to a healthier, slimmer, happier you. The plan will help you lose weight, keep it off, and avoid a host of chronic diseases. This 28-day Mediterranean diet plan is easy to follow because it's filled with easy recipes and diet guidelines. Foods are simple to prepare, delicious, and completely versatile to appeal to your individual taste buds. This style of food is low in processed sugar; is full of fresh, nutrient-dense foods; and doesn't break the bank. And this plan allows you to be creative while still enjoying the foods you like—in moderation. You won't get bored, and you'll never feel like you are on a "diet"—these are all important to a successful long-term lifestyle adaptation.

I'm excited for you, so let's start building your toolbox for success!

PART 1

Getting Started

Your Mediterranean Diet Primer

If you have tried to lose weight before and failed, you are not alone. As a dietitian, I hear stories almost daily from people who have tried diet after diet only to gain the weight back. This 28-day Mediterranean diet is not a fad diet. It is a plan for life.

That said, it is understandable that most people want a quick fix, and in the search for rapid results, they fail. This plan shares time-tested Mediterranean customs relating to nutrition as well as exercise, with an approach proven successful, to set you on a winning course for life.

Pitfalls of the Standard American Diet

Despite the many healthy choices available to us, the standard American diet has historically placed little emphasis on fresh fruits, vegetables, or whole grains. While whole foods are gaining attention for their benefits, our "go-go" society, as a whole, relies far too heavily on processed foods, refined carbohydrates, fried and fast foods, red meats, sugars, high-fat dairy products, saturated and trans fats, and sodium. Such a diet, often devoid of whole grains, fruits, and vegetables, can lead to deficiencies in fiber, vitamins, minerals, and other nutrients essential to good health and even proper functioning of the body.

The standard American diet also includes chemicals, such as high-fructose corn syrup, trans fats, hydrogenated oils, white sugar, bleached and enriched flours, food dyes, and artificial flavors to name a few. These chemicals can increase the risk of health problems.

Data shows that in the United States:

+ More than 2 in 3 adults are considered to be overweight or obese.

+ More than 1 in 3 adults are considered to be obese.

+ More than 1 in 20 adults are considered to have extreme obesity.

Consequently, people who are obese are at increased risk for many serious diseases and health conditions, including high blood pressure, high LDL cholesterol, low HDL cholesterol or high levels of triglycerides, type 2 diabetes, coronary heart disease, stroke, gallbladder disease, osteoarthritis, sleep apnea and breathing problems, some cancers, mental illness, and body pain and difficulty with physical functioning.

Beneath the fast-food propensity of American society lurks a culprit. This culprit is stress, born of a must-do, checklist-based mentality. Stress muddles our priorities as whole foods from nature are traded in for quick fixes from a vending machine or drive-through. Unfortunately, the same holds true for exercise. American society dictates we get as much done as possible in a hurry, which can leave us forgetting the last time we made a conscious decision to take the stairs.

The Mediterranean Diet & Weight Loss

Researchers conclude that a healthy diet and physical activity are essential to getting in shape. The 28-day Mediterranean diet does exactly that, targeting a combination of nutrition and exercise. "Mediterranean diet" refers to common dietary habits among countries that border the Mediterranean Sea. Although diets differ among these regions and countries, as a whole the traditional Mediterranean diet emphasizes fresh fruits and vegetables, whole grains, beans, nuts, seeds, and spices. The main source of fat in the Mediterranean diet is olive oil, a healthy monounsaturated fat. Poultry and dairy products such as cheese and yogurt are consumed in moderate amounts, and fish and seafood are eaten regularly. Red meat is eaten only on occasion.

This abundance of fresh foods translates to few hydrogenated oils and vast amounts of nutrients that benefit the body. In the Mediterranean, most fat intake comes from olive oil, nuts, and fish, which provide large quantities of beneficial omega-3 fatty acids. Spices are used often and generously, so salt is not a necessary seasoning. These collective factors work to lower cholesterol and blood pressure, reducing the risk of heart disease.

Many studies around the world have tested the Mediterranean diet's effectiveness with regard to weight loss. A Harvard study showed that the Mediterranean diet is superior to other weight-loss diets, including low-fat, low-carb diets, and even diets created by major health organizations. Another, the PREDIMED study (PREvención con DIeta MEDiterránea), found that body weight decreased in the study group of those consuming a Mediterranean diet. Research has also shown that this type of eating can reduce the risk for developing certain diseases and cancers and improve the health of individuals with diabetes.

Eat Like a Mediterranean

Kali orexi! That's "bon appétit" at a Greek table, where dining is a cause for celebration. The Mediterranean diet traditionally includes fruits, vegetables, pasta, and rice. As an example, Greeks eat very little red meat, but average nine servings a day of antioxidant-rich fruits and vegetables. Red meat is consumed only a few times a month, but Mediterraneans enjoy fish and poultry several times a week.

The grains consumed in the Mediterranean region are typically whole grains and usually contain very few unhealthy fats. Bread is an important part of this diet, but it is usually eaten plain or dipped in olive oil. Olive oil is also used for cooking, as is canola oil. Butter is not typically used. Mediterranean cooking uses a lot of herbs and spices instead of salt.

Nuts are another mainstay of the Mediterranean diet. Although they are high in fat, most of the fat is unsaturated. They're also high in calories, but a handful a day packs a valuable nutrition and energy punch.

Water remains integral to most any diet, and the Mediterranean diet is no exception. Water goes hand in hand with the active lifestyle in the Mediterranean. Red wine can be enjoyed in moderation if desired. Beyond the food and drink, the traditional Mediterranean meal experience emphasizes the camaraderie of family or friends sharing the celebration.

Live Like a Mediterranean

Mediterranean people tend to be very active, but it's not something they purposely seek out, like in a gym membership—it's simply part of their lifestyle. Cultural differences, such as not having to rely on cars, and walking or biking for transportation, make for a naturally active lifestyle that boosts overall health. These people walk to the market, to visit friends and families, to their jobs, or just to take a stroll. Mediterraneans also possess a traditional love for nature—a trait that shines through in their produce-rich diet. They tend to spend a great

THE MEDITERRANEAN DIET PYRAMID

As illustrated in the pyramid, fresh fruits and vegetables, grains such as whole-wheat bread, pasta, or rice, and olive oil are important parts of every meal. Foods enjoyed daily include nuts, cheese, or yogurt, and red wine. Fish, eggs, poultry, and legumes are consumed several times a week, and meat is restricted to a few times a month.

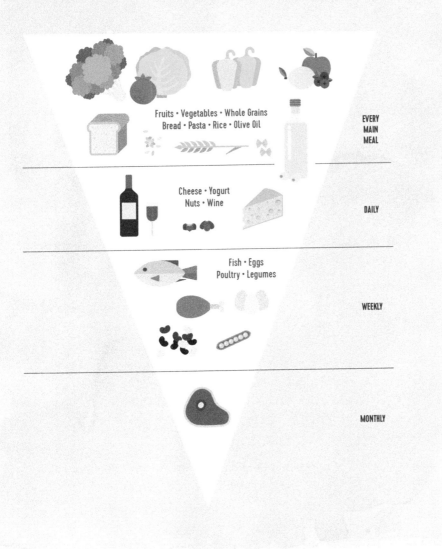

Fruits • Vegetables • Whole Grains
Bread • Pasta • Rice • Olive Oil

EVERY MAIN MEAL

Cheese • Yogurt
Nuts • Wine

DAILY

Fish • Eggs
Poultry • Legumes

WEEKLY

MONTHLY

deal of time outdoors, an easy task in the region's temperate climate, and this naturally lends itself to a healthy lifestyle.

Americans are more likely to join a gym and schedule their activities. Most geographic areas of the United States, for example, are widespread and not conducive to commuting on foot. Americans tend to drive everywhere. But this aside, many Americans spend the bulk of their time indoors. Screen time is inordinate; it's not uncommon for a person to work in front of a computer screen all day without getting up even once or twice to stretch. No wonder we feel like broken lawn chairs at the end of the day—stiff, sore, and not at all inclined to work out afterward.

This diet focuses on the tremendous impact that even a small amount of regular exercise can have on the metabolism and consequently, the ability to lose weight, keep it off, and feel great!

Kick-Start Your Mediterranean Diet

The Mediterranean diet has been undertaken by people all around the world with great success. This diet contributes to weight loss, maintenance of healthy weight, and improved overall health by swapping out bad fats for nutrient-dense foods and making simple lifestyle adjustments.

Together we'll explore the basics of the Mediterranean diet, including how it relates to nutrition, exercise, and portion control, and how you can easily apply it to your lifestyle. You'll learn how to shop and cook like a true *yiayia*. And although this book contains many Mediterranean specialties, you'll quickly see that this cooking style isn't so foreign. At its roots, the Mediterranean diet is about whole foods that come from the earth and are available in most grocery stores. It's not exotic cooking—it's good, healthy cooking!

2

Tackling Weight Loss

For many people, the word diet is synonymous with deprivation. Thoughts of being hungry and missing out while watching others enjoy food can take the steam right out of your resolve to lose weight. There is no sacrifice with the Mediterranean diet—in fact, with its emphasis on feel-good ingredients and robust flavors, you may find yourself enjoying food more than ever before.

Left: Yogurt with Blueberries, Honey, and Mint, p. 90

How Weight Loss Works

Despite all the diet strategies out there, weight management still comes down to "calories in versus calories out." Fad diets may promise that avoiding carbs or eating a soup full of cabbage is the secret to losing weight, but if you want to shed those pounds, it ultimately comes down to eating fewer calories than you burn.

Identifying Your Daily Caloric Intake

Calories are the energy in food. Our bodies constantly demand energy and need the calories from food to function. Energy from calories fuels our actions, whether we're walking, driving a car, or just breathing.

Nutrients such as carbohydrates, fats, and proteins contain calories and are the body's main energy sources. The calories we eat either convert to physical energy or get stored within our body as fat. If you want to lose weight, you can use these calories by reducing your caloric intake and drawing on these reserves for energy, or by increasing your physical activity and burning more calories than you consume.

Because 3,500 calories equals about 1 pound of fat, to lose 1 pound you need to burn 3,500 calories more than you take in.

So, in general, if you cut 500 calories from your typical diet each day, you'd lose about 1 pound a week (500 calories × 7 days = 3,500 calories). If you cut 1,000 calories a day, you would lose 2 pounds per week (1,000 calories × 7 = 7,000 calories).

An average woman needs to eat about 2,000 calories per day to maintain her weight, and 1,500 calories per day to lose 1 pound per week. An average man needs 2,500 calories to maintain his weight and 2,000 calories to lose 1 pound per week. This number can vary depending on factors including age, height, current weight, activity level, metabolic health, and more.

In my practice, I typically find that most people eat many more calories than they think they are eating. When asked to keep a food log, they often are amazed at how many extra calories they consume without thinking about it.

All Calories Are Not Created Equal

While you're losing weight on a limited-calorie daily meal plan, a balanced and nutritious variety of foods is integral to getting all the important nutrients. It's important to note that 1,800 calories, for example, is not the same no matter what foods you eat. Focusing your attention on quality food and beverage choices ensures you get the most mileage from flavor, nutrition, and sustained energy. Some nutrients and foods specifically linked to weight loss include:

PROTEIN. Protein builds and repairs cells throughout the body. Additionally, increased protein intake has been positively associated with weight loss. According to a study published in the *American Journal of Clinical Nutrition*, increasing daily protein intake to account for 30 percent of your calories can reduce the total amount of calories you'll eat over the course of the day. This is because protein tends to be filling and takes a long time to digest. Good sources of protein include beef, chicken, fish, turkey, pork, and tofu. Other sources of protein that fit well in the Mediterranean diet include quinoa, peas, nuts, beans, broccoli, and seeds.

ALL ABOUT BMI AND BMR

Body mass index (BMI) is a measurement system to determine your weight to height proportion. It can help you see where you stand as you begin to formulate your weight-loss goals. To calculate your BMI, go to Webmd.com/diet /body-bmi-calculator.

The body needs a set number of calories just to stay alive and function normally. Your basal metabolic rate (BMR) is the amount of calories your body requires to perform life-sustaining functions, such as keeping your heart beating, breathing, and digesting food. These functions account for the largest amount of calories burned each day. Basically, BMR measures your metabolism or the amount of calories your body burns at rest. To calculate your BMR, visit Calculator.net /bmr-calculator.

FATS. Recent research shows that including good fats (e.g., those high in omega-3 fatty acids) in your diet can actually help you lose weight and keep it off. In fact, the Harvard School of Public Health recommends that about 20 percent of your daily calorie intake comes from healthy fat sources. These include nuts, such as almonds, walnuts, and hazelnuts, and seeds such as pumpkin, sunflower, and flax. Other good sources of healthy fat include avocado, oily fish such as salmon and anchovies, and olive oil.

CARBOHYDRATES. Most Americans exceed their daily intake of carbs, which can lead to weight gain. The recommended daily intake of carbohydrates is about 40 percent of your total calories. Healthy sources include whole grains, such as quinoa and brown rice. Some other good choices, but not usually thought of as carbs, are fruits and starchy vegetables such as sweet potato and butternut squash.

VEGETABLES. The Mediterranean diet emphasizes vegetables in part because they are rich in nutrients, but also because they cook up deliciously through a variety of methods. They're also loaded with fiber, which fills you up, aids in digestion, and keeps you healthy and satiated. Vegetables are a crucial part of this plan and should be enjoyed in abundance every day.

The benefits of maintaining a healthy weight far exceed just looking better. With a lighter load to bear and good nutrition fueling your body's systems, your overall quality of life will improve in more ways than you ever dreamed!

A Holistic Approach

In today's fast-paced culture, we tend to focus on convenience, especially in how we eat. Processed convenience foods are easier and often more readily available than whole foods, but they're not healthy—and they're often misleading with regard to their labels, serving sizes, and ingredients. It may be cheaper and more convenient to eat like this, but the cost to our health is detrimental. There's a saying: "Pay for it now, or pay for it later." With obesity and disease on the rise, there's no better time than now to become mindful of how we tend to our bodies. We are learning more and more about the benefits of healthy eating, and how it can even slow the aging process.

As you can see, the Mediterranean diet is more than just a weight-loss plan. It is a proven, holistic approach to tackling weight-loss goals while creating a path to profound lifestyle changes. Holistic medicine approaches a person as a whole being, addressing the root causes of a problem rather than merely treating symptoms. As a result, a holistic approach can help you achieve meaningful, long-term weight loss in addition to new and informed lifestyle habits and philosophies.

Nutrition

The Mediterranean diet plan focuses on eating heathy food as close to its natural state as possible for optimal health. Take, for example, an apple. An apple is an apple. Applesauce is a step removed but a world away—the skin is removed, and with it all that fiber, which is replaced by added sugar. Then there's apple juice, which is filled with even more sugar. You can see how quickly the best of a food product is stripped away through even the simplest processing.

The hallmark of this plan is unrefined, unprocessed foods that promote wellness. As a dietitian, I believe that food is not only fuel, but also medicine for the body. If we follow a diet such as the Mediterranean plan—rich in nutrients, complex carbohydrates, fruit, vegetables, and good fats—we'll be rewarded with countless health benefits.

"Eating the rainbow" is a popular concept. Its merit lies in the fact that many varieties of produce contain certain nutrients based on their color. For example, orange-colored produce, such as carrots, sweet potatoes, melon, apricots, and mangos, contains abundant amounts of vitamins A and C for vision and immune strength. Berries contain beneficial antioxidants, among other key nutrients. Leafy greens are just all-around nutritional powerhouses. The list goes on, but the point is made: Fill your plate with a variety of foods and colors, and you will reap a variety of rewards.

QUIETING SELF-JUDGMENTS

All of us have self-doubt at some point. Many of us have tried to do things only to realize they weren't for us. Anytime we begin a new challenge, thoughts of doubt may race through our minds, as we ask ourselves questions like, *Can I? Should I?* and *What if . . . ?* Let's talk about developing the spirit and the mind to help get us through this self-doubt with a winning attitude.

By using mindfulness, that is, living in and for the present moment, we step outside ourselves and can become an observer of the thoughts, worries, and doubts lingering in our minds. We can then choose to react to them or ignore them. When starting a health plan, like anything else, it's natural to feel some anxiety. We can use mindfulness to turn those thoughts into more positive ones.

Here are some mindfulness techniques for dissolving self-doubt:

BREATHE. Learning how to breathe properly can help relax you in any situation, wherever you are. I recommend breathing for 3 to 5 minutes in the morning before you get out of bed. This sets a peaceful tone for the day. You can do this at any time that works for you. To focus, try counting your inhales and exhales.

BECOME STILL. Stop and pause for a moment. Simply sit down or stand still, and take a deep breath in. Release it and do this two more times. Try to feel the air entering and leaving your body.

FACE YOUR FEARS. If you have doubts, do not pretend they're not there. Observe the self-doubt. When we face something head on, it's empowering as we often realize it's not as scary as we thought.

FIND SOLID GROUND IN REALITY. Once we acknowledge this doubt is not our reality, but just a manifestation of our imagination, we can conquer it. It is liberating to challenge the defeating dialogue of our mind by focusing on a more positive and realistic outlook.

As you get better at mindfulness, you'll become more in tune with your thoughts and how they affect you. As you continue to face and address them, the doubt and negativity begin to lose their power over you. You're in charge here, and you're going to do great things!

Exercise

Physical activity is a core component of holistic weight loss. Exercise does more than just burn calories. It changes your chemistry, releases powerful neurotransmitters, strengthens and revitalizes muscles, increases energy, and contributes to happiness and a sense of well-being. This is research-based information, and I believe any attempt at weight loss is incomplete without it. For best success, in developing your workout regimen, find a routine that addresses your unique needs, that challenges you appropriately, and—most important—that you truly enjoy. And if over time you find it's getting old, invent a new regimen. Finding the joy in taking care of yourself is the key to a long-lasting exercise ritual.

Rest and Relaxation

Rest is the time our bodies need to regroup, regenerate, and rebuild. There is actually major activity going on in our bodies while we sleep. However, despite the fact that the average adult needs eight hours of sleep a night, the Centers for Disease Control and Prevention (CDC) reports that about 30 percent of Americans are operating on fewer than six hours of sleep a night. This can have detrimental effects on your body—after all, it didn't have enough time to sufficiently revital-ize. But there's more.

For starters, when we're sleep-deprived we tend to crave carbohydrates. Part of the reason is because we're tired, and our brains and bodies want quick energy—enter junk food. Another issue is that sleep depri-vation reduces the functions of leptin, a hormone produced by fat cells. As such, we're just hungrier, crave simple carbs, and of course just want to get to the end of the day so we can sleep.

It's best to shoot for eight hours of restful, quality sleep each night. Of course, this is not always possible, so on those occasions, soothing the mind and body with naps, deep breathing exercises, and meditation can help.

Mindfulness

Why are you here today? What are you hoping to achieve? Let's think about your goals. We know that maintaining a healthy weight feels and looks good, helps ward off disease, and results in a higher quality of life. We've explored how weight and health are largely dependent on diet and exercise, and that other factors, such as rest, can make us healthier and happier and enable us to make better decisions. This is where mindfulness comes in. Your body is most likely to cooperate if your brain is in the game—be sure to include it in your planning!

Consider the following: How can you eat in a healthier way? Do you exercise enough? How can you improve your exercise? What factors— physical, psychological, social—contribute to your diet and exercise regimen? Are you stuck in any unhealthy patterns? What support do you need to overcome these challenges? When you find the answers to these questions, you can avoid issues that prevent you from achieving success. A realistic mind-set and thoughtful approach will help ensure your commitment to long-term weight loss.

As your diet progresses you may find yourself having good days and bad. You may give in to a less healthy craving—this is natural, and it's not a deal breaker. Remember, you are working to develop a new life-style; this doesn't happen overnight—it happens over time. Be kind and patient with yourself, but definitely pat yourself on the back for "good behavior"! Your positive mind-set will take over as the default when you make a ritual out of kindness, patience, and self-empowerment.

Portion Control

When we diet, we seek to lose fat, but it isn't that simple; we usually lose a combination of fat, lean tissue, and water. Also, over time with changes that occur in the body as a result of weight loss, we may reach a point at which we need to decrease our calorie intake further to continue weight loss. Whether you are starting a new diet or cutting calories to meet your body's changing needs, you can be sure you're making the most of your portions through a few simple measures:

CHOOSE WISELY. Avoid high-calorie, low-nutrition items. These hijack your calorie count with nothing to show for it. Make every calorie count by planning ahead and choosing wisely. Swap high-calorie foods for lower-calorie options, and conversely, make sure any high-calorie foods you enjoy are nutrient rich (think nuts, avocado, peanut butter).

SHIFT YOUR PLATE'S CONTENTS. Crowd out meat and carbohydrates with generous portions of vegetables. A good diet should not be about deprivation; rather it should shift the attention toward foods and recipes that are more health supportive and sustaining.

START SMALL. At the beginning of a meal, take slightly less than what you think you'll eat. You can have seconds if you're still truly hungry.

EAT FROM PLATES, NOT PACKAGES. Eating directly from a container gives you no sense of how much you're eating. Seeing food on a plate or in a bowl keeps you aware of how much you're eating.

CHECK FOOD LABELS. Begin a habit of reading the Nutrition Facts panel on packages, especially the ingredients, serving size, and number of calories per serving. You may find that the small bag of chips you eat with lunch every day is two servings, not one, which means you've been consuming twice the calories you originally thought you were.

DINE OUT SMARTLY. Restaurant portions tend to be enormous and high in sodium and fats. To compensate, choose to split the meal with a friend, or eat half at the restaurant and bring the leftovers home for a future meal. Seek restaurants that offer healthy options, or look for menu options that might be labeled as light fare or low calorie. Ask for dressing on the side so you can dip your food, or bring your own dressing.

USE A CALORIE COUNTER. Check out reputable resources that offer tools to count calories, such as websites or smartphone applications. One to try is the SuperTracker at ChooseMyPlate.gov.

SERVING SIZES FOR COMMON FOODS

It can be helpful—and eye opening—to be aware of the portions you eat. Here are some serving size guidelines to follow:

EQUIVALENT			FOOD	CALORIES
Fist		¾ cup	Rice	150
			Pasta	150
			Potatoes	150
Palm		4 ounces	Lean meat	160
			Fish	160
			Poultry	160
Handful		1 ounce	Nuts	170
			Raisins	85
Thumb		1 ounce	Peanut butter	170
			Hard cheese	100

Identify Bad Habits

We are all creatures of habit. Most of us buy the same things, cook the same recipes, and keep the same snacks in our home over time. It's important to remember that actions become habits, and by continuing the same good or bad patterns week after week, we set ourselves up either to succeed or fail with our weight-loss goals, depending on our habits. We may have habits so comfortable we can't imagine life without them. In my experience, anybody starting a diet is more likely to be successful if they change their habits slowly, one step at a time. Some common traps I have seen dieters fall into include:

DRINKING THEIR CALORIES. Lattes and sugary drinks add up to hundreds of extra calories.

EATING WHEN NOT HUNGRY/SNACKING OUT OF BOREDOM. Hobbies and distractions come in handy here.

EXCEEDING PORTIONS. This is especially true with carbs, snacks, and packaged goods.

JUSTIFYING "SALAD." A salad laden with starches, cheese, dried fruit, nuts, and dressings can blow the calorie budget.

EATING TOO MUCH OF A GOOD THING. Moderation matters even with healthy foods, especially those with higher calorie counts such as nuts, oils, and avocado.

GIVING UP. It's okay not to be perfect. You are creating new habits and this takes time.

Since habits evolve over time, this 28-day Mediterranean diet provides a weekly Habit Tracker (page 50) to help keep you on course. This tool will help increase your awareness of behaviors and patterns that may be helping or hindering your success.

THE BALANCED PLATE

Being on a diet doesn't have to mean an empty plate. Go ahead—fill your plate! But before you start scooping, picture *how* you will fill your plate. A balanced plate—one that provides the right ratio of foods—looks like this:

Good protein sources include poultry, fish, and lean meat that are grilled, baked, or broiled.

Some starches include peas, corn, beans, pasta, bread, alcohol, potato, sweet potato, butternut squash, and quinoa and other whole grains.

Be extra mindful of portions of what I call "calorically dense" foods: avocado, oils, nuts, and nut butters. Even though these contain healthy fats and are good for us, they're high in calories. Reasonable portion sizes would be one-fourth of an avocado, 1 tablespoon nut butter or oil, and 10 to 15 nuts.

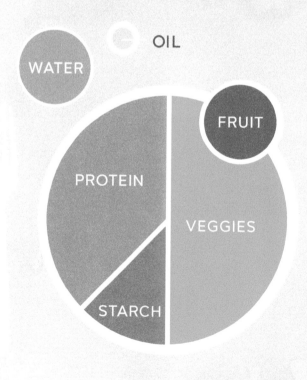

Set Goals

Goals are important for success. Realistic, well-planned weight-loss goals keep you focused and motivated. They provide a plan for change as you transition to a healthier lifestyle.

But not all goals are helpful. Unrealistic and overly aggressive weight-loss goals can undermine your efforts and leave you feeling frustrated. The following tips will help you create goals that will help you reduce weight and improve your overall health.

Focus on Process Goals

Goals for weight loss can focus on either outcomes or process. An outcome goal—what you hope to achieve in the end—might be to lose a certain amount of weight. While this goal may give you a target, it doesn't address how you will reach it.

A process goal is a necessary step to achieving a desired outcome. For example, a process goal might be eating five helpings of fruits or vegetables a day, walking 30 minutes a day, or drinking water at every meal. Process goals can be particularly helpful for weight loss because they focus on changing behaviors and habits necessary for losing weight.

Set SMART Goals

A good goal-setting strategy is to follow the SMART goal checklist. Consider whether your weight-loss goals—process goals or outcome goals—meet the following criteria:

SPECIFIC. A good goal includes specific details. For example, a goal to exercise more is not specific, but a goal to walk 20 minutes during your lunch break is specific. You are saying what you will do, how long you will do it, and when you will do it.

YOUR PERSONALIZED WEIGHT-LOSS PLAN

Keeping a journal and engaging in other self-monitoring techniques can help make you more aware of what you're eating, and why. Sometimes merely seeing a list of everything you consume throughout the course of a day can prevent trips to the kitchen. Such techniques hold you accountable and let you reflect on what's working or not working. Here are two charts designed to help you keep records of your goals and daily outcomes. You can customize these charts, adding categories that matter most to you.

MY BODY GOALS		
	CURRENT	DESIRED
Weight		
Natural waist (in inches)		
Hips (in inches)		
Upper arms		
Chest		
Thighs (at widest point)		

MY DAILY GOALS		
	YES/NO	COMMENT
Did I eat enough fruits and vegetables?		
Did I try a new protein?		
Did I feel good mentally today?		
Did I feel physically good today?		
Did I have any outstanding issues or events that impacted my diet?		
Did I get a good night's sleep?		
Did I exercise?		

MEASURABLE. If you can measure a goal, you can determine how successful you are at meeting the goal. A goal of eating better is not easily measured, but a goal of eating 1,500 calories a day can be. A goal of walking is not measurable, but it's measurable if your goal is to walk for 30 minutes four days a week.

ATTAINABLE. An attainable goal denotes you have sufficient time and resources to achieve it. For example, if your schedule doesn't allow spending an hour at the gym every day, it's not an attainable goal. However, one weekday trip and two weekend trips to the gym might be attainable. Your mode of exercise should also be attainable in that it is something you can do and enjoy doing (walking, swimming, using exercise equipment).

REALISTIC. Goals should be realistic. It is certainly possible to lose 100 pounds or more if the need and resolve are there, but for most people, a realistic outcome goal is to lose 5 to 10 percent of their current weight. Setting an unrealistic goal, particularly when starting out, may result in disappointment or giving up altogether. Keep in mind that goals can be expanded as your dietary success gains momentum.

TRACKABLE. Keeping track can help you evaluate your progress and stay motivated. If you have an outcome goal of losing 20 pounds, record your weight each week. If your goal is to eat 1,500 calories a day, keep a food diary.

Exercise, Rest, *and* Relaxation

In this chapter, we take a closer look at a key component in health—exercise. I also expand on rest and relaxation as they pertain to wellness. All three components are incorporated into the 28-day Mediterranean diet plan, and you'll learn how they play a significant role in success.

Regular Exercise

Research shows that being physically active is one of the most important things you can do for your health. According to the CDC, physical activity can help control weight; reduce the risk of heart disease, diabetes, and cancers; strengthen bones, muscles, and mobility; improve mental health; and lead to a longer life.

Exercise plays an important role in the 28-day Mediterranean diet plan because it will help you feel more energetic and help burn the calories you are eating more efficiently. On this plan, we will gradually build up to the recommendations listed on page 31. Ideally, a regimen of 30 minutes of cardio 4 days a week is optimal. However, if you have never exercised before, feel like you have no time, or are timid about starting, don't fret. Every bit counts, so it's okay to start slowly. Sometimes, 10 minutes a day is all you need to jump-start your motivation to do more.

I always tell my patients that you don't have to run a marathon. Just start somewhere. If walking around the parking lot at work is an option, start there. If you can get to the gym on the weekends, do that. If you have a treadmill at home collecting dust, clean it off and hop on for 15 minutes while making a call or watching your favorite television show. Decide what is best for you and work it into your schedule. To hold yourself accountable, write it on your calendar like any other important date. Over time, you can gradually increase your workouts.

Exercise should include a combination of aerobic (cardio) and muscle-strengthening activities. Both the American Heart Association and World Health Organization recommend 30 minutes of moderate aerobic activity 5 days per week, or 25 minutes of vigorous aerobic activity 3 days per week, or a combination. They also recommend strengthening activities at least 2 days per week for additional health benefits. Individuals who wish to lower their blood pressure or cholesterol should get 40 minutes of aerobic activity at least 3 times a week. Do not let the statistics muddle your brain, though. Every minute spent working your body helps.

Getting the Most out of Your Workouts

Fitting regular exercise into your daily schedule may seem difficult at first. The key is to find the right exercise for you. It should be one you enjoy.

Cardio workouts are extremely important for any weight-loss and health plan. No matter what type of cardio you do, here are some tips for getting the most out of your workouts:

MIX IT UP WITH INTERVAL TRAINING. You'll burn more calories by alternating between a few minutes at a regular pace and a few minutes going faster. You will also build endurance.

USE YOUR ARMS. Many forms of cardio are all about the legs, so whenever possible, maximize your cardio time by focusing on working your arms as well. While walking or running, raise your arms up and down above your head or swinging them to the side. If you can, try to work your arms while on a treadmill or elliptical.

GO A LITTLE BIT LONGER. If you are doing 30 minutes, try doing 5 or 10 minutes more. You'd be surprised how many more calories you burn by pushing yourself a little longer—and you'll feel so empowered!

INCORPORATE STRENGTH TRAINING. Use inclines whenever possible and carry or wear light weights when walking.

CHANGE IT UP. Get more out of your cardio workouts by including three or more different varieties each week. Walk for a few minutes and move to the elliptical or bike. This enables you to work different muscle groups and keep the routine fresh and interesting.

CHALLENGE YOURSELF. Find other ways to make your cardio workout harder. If you bike, stand instead of resting. If you're in a class, try the more intensive movements.

Getting started is the hardest part of exercise. Once you're going, try to give it all you've got. When you are done with your workout, you will feel great.

EXERCISE MYTHS

Many people think they have to lift heavy weights or run miles to lose weight. There are many myths out there, so let's dispel a few to assist us in our wellness journey:

MYTH: GETTING OFF THE COUCH CANNOT HELP YOU LOSE WEIGHT. By reducing activities that keep you sedentary, like watching television or playing computer games, you'll move more. By simply standing more, you are moving more. For 30 minutes each night, try not to watch television—get up from the table after dinner and do something—anything! This activity burns more calories than sitting.

MYTH: YOU MUST EXERCISE FOR 45 MINUTES TO SEE RESULTS. Studies show that more is not always better. Even 5 minutes of exercise is far better than none. And 30 minutes a day is enough to markedly reduce your risk of certain diseases and lose weight.

MYTH: THE MORE YOU SWEAT, THE MORE YOU BURN. Sweating is merely our body's way of cooling down and has little to do with how many calories we burn. If you are raising your heart rate more than you ordinarily would, you're burning calories, sweat or no sweat.

MYTH: LIFTING HEAVY WEIGHTS IS THE KEY TO BEING FIT. Strength training is an important part of physical fitness, but it's only one component. A combination of diet, cardiovascular exercise, and strength training helps people achieve optimal fitness levels.

Set a Routine

Aerobic and strengthening activities work differently, but both are important for weight loss and good health. Aerobic, or cardio, activity increases our heart rate and blood circulation through the body. It also releases endorphins, a feel-good hormone. Walking, jogging, running, biking, swimming, rowing, elliptical use, and stair climbing are some of the more common cardio exercises that raise metabolic rates and burn calories.

Strength training, much like cardio, helps strengthen your heart and improves blood flow. It also strengthens your core, builds muscle, increases bone density, and more. This is good news for dieters, especially because muscle mass burns more calories than body fat, even at rest. It is important to strengthen muscles, but it is even more important to strengthen your core. Push-ups, sit-ups, walking lunges, Pilates exercises, and repetitions using weights are just a few strength exercises you can use to work your core and muscles.

Scheduling both cardio and strength exercises in your workout routine will help you reap optimum results! The following is a four-week sample exercise recommendation table you can follow or fill in with an exercise plan that works for you. This particular plan includes 30 minutes of cardio activity 4 times weekly, along with an increasing buildup of strength-training exercises (see page 32). After the first 4 weeks, you can maintain a regular pattern of cardio and core exercise.

WEEK	MONDAY	TUESDAY	WEDNESDAY	THURSDAY	FRIDAY	SATURDAY	SUNDAY
Week 1	Cardio	Cardio & Strength	REST	Cardio & Strength	REST	Cardio	REST
Week 2	Cardio & Strength	Cardio	REST	Cardio & Strength	REST	Cardio & Optional Strength	REST
Week 3	Cardio & Strength	Cardio	REST	Cardio & Optional Strength	REST	Cardio & Strength	REST
Week 4	Cardio & Strength	Cardio	REST	Cardio & Strength	REST	Cardio & Optional Strength	REST

Strength-Training Exercises

For your strength-training workout, choose one exercise each from the A, B, C, and D groups and perform 2 to 3 rounds of 8 to 10 repetitions per exercise. Make sure to choose different workouts from each group for each day of the week. This combination results in a total body workout that can be done either twice a week or, optimally, three times a week.

Here are some samples for days that call for strength training:

#1 Sample Strength Training Day

Group A (Core): Bicycle Crunches: 2 to 3 sets of 8 to 10 repetitions each set

Group B (Upper Body): Triceps Dips: 2 to 3 sets of 8 to 10 repetitions each set

Group C (Lower Body): Squats: 2 to 3 sets of 8 to 10 repetitions each set

Group D (Full Body): Jumping Jacks: 2 to 3 sets of 8 to 10 repetitions each set

#2 Sample Strength Training Day

Group A (Core): Plank: 2 to 3 sets of 8 to 10 repetitions each set

Group B (Upper Body): Arm Circles: 2 to 3 sets of 8 to 10 repetitions each set

Group C (Lower Body): Lunges: 2 to 3 sets of 8 to 10 repetitions each set

Group D (Full Body): Burpees: 2 to 3 sets of 8 to 10 repetitions each set

Group A: Core

PLANK

Start on the floor on all fours. Place your hands directly under your shoulders, and knees directly under your hips. Find a neutral spine position, brace your abs, and push off your knees. Your torso should form a straight line from your head to your feet. Set your gaze at a point on the floor about a foot in front of you, and make sure your neck is in line with the rest of your body. Breathe, as you hold this position for 8 to 10 seconds. This counts as one repetition.

BICYCLE CRUNCH

Start on the floor lying on your back. Bring your knees to your chest and interlace your fingers behind your neck. Lift your shoulders off the floor, tighten your abdominal muscles, and tuck your chin into your chest. Twist, to touch the inside of your right arm to the inside of your left thigh while straightening your right leg. Twist to touch the inside of your left arm to the inside of your right thigh while straightening your left leg. This counts as one repetition.

HOLLOW ROCK

Start on the floor lying your back. Contract your abs while pressing the small of your back into the floor. With your legs straight, raise them off the floor a couple of inches. Straighten your arms above your head, and raise them off the floor a couple of inches. Keeping your lower back on the floor and abs engaged, rock back and forth on your sitz bones. This counts as one repetition.

Group B: Upper Body

PUSH-UP

Start on the floor on all fours. Place your hands directly under your shoulders, and knees directly under your hips. Find a neutral spine position, brace your abs, and push off your knees. Set your gaze at a point on the floor about a foot in front of you, and make sure your neck is in line with the rest of your body. Draw your shoulder blades back and down your back, while keeping the elbows close to your body. Lower your body until your chest touches the floor. Making sure the abs and glutes are still engaged, exhale, and push yourself up, in one straight line, to the starting position. *If this is too challenging, keep your knees on the floor while performing the push-up.*

ARM CIRCLES

Start standing with your arms extended straight out by your sides. Arms should be parallel to the floor, with your body forming a "T" shape. Brace your abs and make clockwise circles with your arms, about 1 foot in diameter. After 15 to 20 seconds, reverse the direction, and make counterclockwise circles. This counts as one repetition.

TRICEPS DIP

Start sitting on the floor in front of a step, bench, or sturdy chair, with knees slightly bent and feet planted firmly on the floor. Grab the edge of the elevated surface behind you, and place your hands slightly wider than hip-width apart. Bend them to a 90-degree angle. Brace your abs and straighten your arms, pushing through your heels. Lower back down to a seated position. This counts as one repetition.

Group C: Lower Body

SQUAT

Start standing with your feet hip-width apart and arms down by your side. Brace your abs and send your hips back as you start bending your knees, descending into a squat. Keep your chest up, looking straight ahead. Go as far down as you can without dropping your chest. Once you reach your depth, spring back into the standing position, squeezing your glutes at the top.

LUNGE

Start by standing with your feet a bit wider than shoulder-width apart. Brace your abs and take a big step forward with your left foot. Make sure your knees, hips, and shoulders all face forward. Keep your chest up, brace your abs, and sink straight down until your left knee makes a 90-degree angle and your right knee is pointing straight down toward the ground. Shift the weight onto the ball of your right foot as you push back up, and step back into the starting position. This counts as one repetition.

WALL SIT

Start standing with your back against a wall. Slowly slide yourself down the wall until your thighs are parallel to the ground, making a 90-degree angle. Make sure your knees are directly above your ankles and keep your back straight. Hold the position for 8 to 10 seconds. This counts as one repetition.

Group D: Full Body

JUMPING JACK

Start standing with your feet together and hands down by your sides. Brace your abs and jump both legs out to the side, landing with your feet just outside your hips and arms overhead. Keep your knees slightly bent while you jump again to bring your feet back together and your arms down to your side. This counts as one repetition.

BURPEE

Start standing with your feet hip-width apart. Lower yourself into a squat. Place your hands on the floor in front of you and shift your weight forward. Jump or walk your feet back into a plank position. Keep your abs braced and make sure your body creates a straight line. Jump or walk your feet back toward your hands, to the bottom of the squat. Jump or stand up. This constitutes one repetition.

Stay Hydrated

Drinking water has long been associated with weight loss and other benefits, and is another important part of the Mediterranean diet plan. To begin with, water makes you feel full and can prevent overeating. Sometimes when we feel hungry we are actually thirsty, so downing a glass of water can quench the thirst that's mimicking hunger. Also, the more water we drink, the less we turn to sugary drinks like soda and juices that can add up to extra calories and halt weight loss. Some studies, including one by the *Annals of Family Medicine*, have linked hydration levels to BMI numbers (see page 13) and obesity.

So how much water is enough? I tell my patients about 8 cups per day. If your urine is bright in color and you tend to be thirsty, you need to drink more. I recommend buying a liter container. Fill it up and, if desired, add lemon, lime, berries, or cucumbers for taste. Sip on it wherever you go and keep track of how often you refill the container so you know exactly how much or little you have taken in. To supplement your water intake, you can also enjoy water-rich fruits and veggies such as cucumbers, watermelon, cantaloupe, celery, apples, and berries, which provide important nutrients to boot. Even teas, broths, and decaf drinks, such as decaf tea or coffee, and seltzer count toward hydration.

Rest and Relaxation

Are you getting enough R&R? Rest and health go hand in hand, but according to the Centers for Disease Control and Prevention, more than 35 percent of people are sleep deprived. With about the same percentage reported as being obese, it makes me wonder, could there be a link?

According to a study by the *Annals of Internal Medicine*, insufficient sleep can reduce the effectiveness of dieting. Dieters in the study were put on different sleep schedules. When they got enough rest, half the weight they lost was from fat. When they did not get adequate sleep, on the same meal plan, that amount of fat was cut in half, and the remaining weight lost was from lean body mass. With less sleep, they were hungrier, less satiated after meals, and less energized. It was found that those on a sleep-deprived diet had a 55 percent reduction in fat loss compared to those who were well rested.

Generally speaking, after a few days of inadequate sleep, your body's ability to produce insulin is disrupted. Consequently, you become more insulin resistant and fats circulate in your blood and create more insulin. This excess insulin ends up storing fat in all the wrong places, such as in organs, resulting in added weight gain and related diseases.

Additional research published in the *Journal of Clinical Endocrinology and Metabolism* found that sleeping for less than 6 hours a night triggers the area of the brain that increases the need for food while depressing the hormones (leptin and ghrelin) that control hunger and willpower. Lack of sleep also activates cortisol, a hormone associated with fat gain and hunger.

Now that we know lack of sleep can affect your appetite, lead to weight gain, and render you too tired to go to the gym, how much sleep is enough? According to the National Institutes of Health, the amount of sleep you need each night changes over the course of your life. Although sleep needs vary, adults generally need about 7 to 8 hours of sleep each night for optimum health.

Relaxation is every bit as critical to good functioning of the body as rest and exercise. As we run through life with our checklists in hand, we put our bodies into the fight-or-flight nervous system. Our bodies were not designed to live in this state for extended periods of time, so it's important to set time aside every day to breathe deeply, unwind, and just "be."

Physically, relaxation lowers heart rate and blood pressure, aids in proper digestion, and reduces muscle tension, among other benefits. Emotionally, relaxation is linked with stress reduction, improved mental health and mood, and more. That said, it can be very beneficial to add some breathing exercises or yoga to your physical activity schedule.

PART 2

Your 28-Day Commitment

The 28-Day Plan

This chapter provides simple menus for the four weeks, as well as tips and guidelines on how to prep the food for each week. Rest assured, you don't need to be a gourmet chef to follow this plan, but you may want to make dishes ahead of time, or chop your vegetables ahead of time—and I'll offer tips for streamlining the process. This chapter takes all the guesswork out of meal preparations.

I also give you easy and delicious snack ideas and suggested timing, as well as recommendations for how much water to drink. Your own "personal trainer" will offer a different workout for each week. You'll be able to track your patterns through an interactive chart that asks you to log your habits weekly.

You read earlier that this is not a fad diet, but a plan for life. I say that because, again, fad diets tend not to be sustainable. The Mediterranean diet plan is backed by science, and it's based in common sense—a variety of good whole foods with an emphasis on nutrition-dense foods. But to be successful, even the best diet requires commitment. Commitment is a huge factor when it comes to losing weight and keeping it off. This is a 28-day plan. Before you start it, take some time to fully commit to the time frame and the plan. Consider all the factors discussed so far, especially your habits and goals.

Every piece of this plan is equally important. The diet, the exercise, the charts, and the tips all go together to create the foundation of your journey to weight loss, weight maintenance, and overall good health.

The meal plans that follow are based on a 1,500- to 1,800-calorie-per-day diet. As you begin, it's important to follow the portions noted in the recipes (so if a recipe says it serves four, split it into four equal servings and only eat one). Everyone's individual caloric needs vary based on a number of metabolic factors and activity levels, so some people may discover the meal plans contain too many calories to lose weight. If this is the case for you, the following steps can help you adjust your calorie intake to a level that helps you lose weight:

- Decrease portion size by one-fourth, so portions would be 75 percent of that listed in the recipes.
- Increase activity levels.
- Eat fewer and/or smaller snacks.

Conversely, if you exercise quite a bit and are losing more than a safe 1 to 2 pounds per week, add 3 ounces lean grilled protein to any vegetarian meals.

A NOTE ABOUT SNACKS: Snacks are okay—just make them count! This plan actually allows for two to three snacks per day if you are hungry. Suggested snacks are provided, but generally, snacks should include 1 ounce of protein—such as an ounce of nuts, two tablespoons of hummus, a tablespoon of nut butter; a half piece of fruit (or half cup of fruit such as berries); and either a cup of nonstarchy vegetables or a half cup of starchy vegetables.

Week 1

You might be following this plan to lose weight, or perhaps you just want to become healthier. Whatever your reason, this first week is all about first steps—and you may feel a mix of excitement and apprehension. This is natural. Once you go food shopping and tackle the prep work on a few recipes, you will feel better equipped to get through this toughest week. Take it one day at a time and be patient as you get into the swing of things. Remember your goals—post them or supportive words on your refrigerator as a reminder. You can do this.

If you are trying to lose weight, weigh yourself on the first day as a benchmark, but wait a week to weigh yourself again.

Prep Ahead

- Hardboil 5 eggs for breakfasts.
- Prepare Greek Salad dressing (page 110).
- Steam brown rice and refrigerate or freeze it in single-serving (½-cup) containers.
- Finely chop red onions and refrigerate them in a well-sealed container (or buy prechopped).
- Make Red Wine Poached Pears (page 198).
- Prepare Hummus (page 100).
- Prepare Baba Ganoush (page 101).

Shopping List

DAIRY AND EGGS

- Almond milk, unsweetened, ½ gallon (can substitute skim milk)
- Cheese, feta, ½ cup
- Cheese, mozzarella, part-skim, 4 ounces
- Cheese, Parmesan, grated, 6 ounces (¾ cup)
- Cream, heavy (whipping), 3 tablespoons
- Eggs, 18
- Yogurt, Greek, unsweetened nonfat plain, 2½ cups

PRODUCE

- Asparagus, 1 pound
- Bananas, 2
- Basil, fresh, 2 bunches
- Bell pepper, red, 1
- Blackberries, 1 pint
- Blueberries, 2 pints
- Broccoli, 1 head
- Carrots, baby, 1 pound
- Cilantro, fresh, 1 small bunch
- Cucumbers, 2
- Dill, fresh, 1 bunch
- Eggplant, 1
- Fennel bulbs, 5
- Fruit (fresh or frozen, your choice), 2 cups
- Garlic, 3 heads
- Ginger, fresh, 1 (3-inch) piece
- Jalapeño pepper, 1
- Lemons, 9
- Lettuce, romaine, 1 head
- Lime, 1
- Mangos, 2
- Mint, fresh, 1 bunch
- Onions, red, 2
- Onions, yellow, 2
- Oranges, 2
- Parsley, fresh, Italian, 3 bunches
- Pears, 5
- Peas, shelled (fresh or frozen), 3 cups
- Raspberries, 1 pint
- Rosemary, fresh, 1 bunch
- Salad greens, 1 (9-ounce) bag
- Scallions, 6
- Shallot, 1
- Strawberries, 1 pint
- Sweet potatoes, 4
- Thyme, fresh, 1 bunch
- Tomatoes, cherry, 2 pints
- Tomatoes, large, 4
- Zucchini, 11

MEAT, POULTRY, AND FISH

- Bacon, turkey, low-sodium, 2 ounces
- Chicken breast, ground, 1 pound
- Chicken breasts, boneless, skinless, 1 pound
- Crabmeat, lump, 1½ pounds
- Pork tenderloin, 1½ pounds
- Salmon, 1½ pounds
- Shrimp, baby (cooked), ½ pound
- Turkey breast, deli-sliced, 3 ounces
- Turkey breast, ground, 1½ pounds

GRAINS

- Bread, whole-wheat, light, 1 loaf
- Brown rice
- Hamburger buns, whole-wheat, 1 package
- Pasta, whole-wheat, 8 ounces
- Pita, whole-wheat, 1 package

CANNED

- Chickpeas, 1 (14-ounce) can
- Tomatoes, chopped, 1 (14-ounce) can
- Tomatoes, crushed, 1 (14-ounce) can
- White beans, 1 (14-ounce) can

OTHER

- Cocoa powder, unsweetened
- Honey, ½ cup
- Mustard, Dijon
- Olive oil, extra-virgin
- Olives, black, 2 cups
- Pine nuts, 2 ounces
- Sunflower seeds, 2 tablespoons (optional)
- Tahini
- Vanilla extract, 1 teaspoon
- Vinegar, balsamic
- Vinegar, red wine
- Walnuts, 4 ounces
- Wine, dry red
- Wine, dry white

PANTRY AND REFRIGERATOR STAPLES

(Check On-Hand Supplies)

- Cayenne pepper
- Cinnamon sticks, 2
- Cumin, ground
- Garlic powder
- Ginger, ground, ½ teaspoon
- Italian seasoning, 2 tablespoons
- Marjoram, dried, 1 tablespoon
- Nonstick cooking spray
- Nutmeg, ground, 1 teaspoon
- Oregano, dried, 1 tablespoon
- Peppercorns
- Red pepper flakes
- Rosemary, dried, 2 tablespoons
- Sea salt
- Lite Italian dressing

Menu

MONDAY

Breakfast
1 hardboiled egg
Chocolate Banana Smoothie (page 87)

Lunch
Greek Salad (page 110)
3 ounces deli turkey

Dinner
Pan-Roasted Salmon with
Gremolata (page 155)
Broccoli with Ginger and
Garlic (page 186)
¼ cup cooked brown rice
3 ounces red wine

Water
8 (8-ounce) glasses throughout the day

Snacks
2 to 3: mid-morning, mid-
afternoon, evening

TUESDAY

Breakfast
1 hardboiled egg
Leftover Chocolate Banana Smoothie

Lunch
Leftover Salmon with Gremolata
Leftover Greek Salad

Dinner
Chicken Gyros with Tzatziki (page 173)
½ whole-wheat pita
Parmesan Zucchini Sticks (page 188)

Water
8 (8-ounce) glasses throughout the day

Snacks
2 to 3: mid-morning, mid-afternoon,
and evening

WEDNESDAY

Breakfast
1 hardboiled egg
Berry and Yogurt Parfait (page 89)

Lunch
Leftover Chicken Gyros with Tzatziki
½ whole-wheat pita
½ cup baby carrots

Dinner
Zucchini Noodles with Peas and
Mint (page 146)
Caprese Salad (page 112)

Water
8 (8-ounce) glasses throughout the day

Snacks
2 to 3: mid-morning, mid-afternoon,
and evening

THURSDAY

Breakfast
1 hardboiled egg
Fruit Smoothie (page 88)

Lunch
Leftover Zucchini Noodles with Peas
and Mint
½ cup cooked brown rice
½ pear

Dinner
Crab Cakes with Shaved Fennel
Salad (page 157)
Sweet Potato Mash (page 127)
Red Wine Poached Pears (page 198)

Water
8 (8-ounce) glasses throughout the day

Snacks
2 to 3: mid-morning, mid-afternoon,
and evening

FRIDAY

Breakfast
1 hardboiled egg
Leftover Fruit Smoothie

Lunch
Leftover Crab Cakes with Shaved
Fennel Salad
Leftover Sweet Potato Mash

Dinner
Turkey Burgers with Mango
Salsa (page 164)
1 whole-wheat hamburger bun
½ cup baby carrots

Water
8 (8-ounce) glasses throughout the day

Snacks
2 to 3: mid-morning, mid-afternoon,
and evening

SATURDAY

Breakfast
Tomato and Zucchini Frittata (page 95)
½ cup sliced strawberries

Lunch
Leftover Turkey Burgers with
Mango Salsa
1 whole-wheat hamburger bun
2 cups salad greens with 2 tablespoons
Lite Italian dressing

Dinner
One-Pan Tuscan Chicken (page 168)
2 ounces cooked whole-wheat pasta
Roasted Asparagus with Lemon and
Pine Nuts (page 183)

Water
8 (8-ounce) glasses throughout the day

Snacks:
2 to 3: mid-morning, mid-afternoon,
and evening

SUNDAY

Breakfast
French Toast (page 94)
½ cup sliced strawberries
2 low-sodium turkey bacon slices

Lunch
Leftover One-Pan Tuscan Chicken
2 ounces cooked whole-wheat pasta
2 cups mixed greens with 2 tablespoons
Greek Salad dressing (page 110)

Dinner
Dijon and Herb Pork
Tenderloin (page 175)
Roasted Fennel with Tomatoes (page 190)
½ cup cooked brown rice
3 ounces dry red wine

Water
8 (8-ounce) glasses throughout the day

Snacks
2 to 3: mid-morning, mid-afternoon,
and evening

SUGGESTED SNACKS
Carrots, ½ cup, and Hummus,
2 tablespoons (page 100)
Date Nut Energy Balls, 1 (page 202)
Carrot and Bran Mini Muffins,
1 to 2 (page 93)
½ apple and 1 tablespoon almond butter
1 hardboiled egg

Your Personal Trainer

The following is your exercise plan for the week. Fill in the table with the cardio and strength-training exercises (see page 32) you plan to do.

M	T	W	TH	F	SAT	S
Cardio:	Cardio: Strength Group A: Group B: Group C: Group D:	REST	Cardio: Strength Group A: Group B: Group C: Group D:	REST	Cardio:	REST

Habit Tracker

It's important to make healthy lifestyle choices in addition to dietary changes. Create a list of healthy habits you want to maintain over the next four weeks and mark the days when you succeed.

HABIT	M	T	W	TH	F	SAT	S
Drank 8 Glasses of Water	X		X	X		X	

Week 2

Congratulations, you made it through Week 1! Take some time to reflect on what worked and what didn't, and consider how you can use this experience to ensure Week 2 goes smoothly and successfully.

Now is the time to add more exercise if you started on the lower end of the recommendations. If you're finding it hard to drink all the water that's recommended, add lemon or cucumber slices to your water for flavor, or try some herbal teas or seltzer. Even water-based fruits and vegetables count (see page 37). If you stumbled, don't be hard on your-self—remember, you are creating new habits and this takes time.

This week should be easier, though, because you have the first week under your belt and are, hopefully, becoming more familiar with journaling and tracking. Glance back at your first week's work and pat yourself on the back for a job well done, as you look forward to another exciting seven days—and enticing new foods!

Prep Ahead

♦ Make Carrot and Bran Mini Muffins (page 93) and refrigerate or freeze.

♦ Scramble 5 eggs and refrigerate or freeze in single-serve containers.

♦ Make White Bean Soup with Kale (page 118) and refrigerate or freeze in single-serve containers.

♦ Make Date Nut Energy Balls (page 202).

♦ Make Lemon and Watermelon Granita (page 196).

♦ Remove the skin and bones from a rotisserie chicken, and chop the meat into 1-cup portions. Freeze in single-serve containers.

♦ Make bread crumbs from left-over whole-wheat bread. Toast the bread, crumble or run it through a food processor, and store in a resealable bag.

Shopping List

DAIRY AND EGGS

- Almond milk, unsweetened, 1 quart (can substitute skim milk)
- Cheese, feta, crumbled, 12 ounces (2¼ cups)
- Cheese, mozzarella, part-skim, grated, 4 ounces
- Cheese, Parmesan, grated, ¼ cup
- Eggs, 2 dozen
- Yogurt, frozen, vanilla, ½ gallon
- Yogurt, Greek, unsweetened nonfat plain, 2¼ cups

PRODUCE

- Apples, 4
- Apple, green, 1
- Avocados, 2
- Basil, fresh, 1 bunch
- Bell peppers, green, 2
- Bell peppers, red, 9
- Blackberries, 1 pint
- Blueberries, 4 pints
- Carrots, 2 pounds
- Cucumbers, 2
- Dill, fresh, 1 bunch
- Eggplant, 1
- Fruit, fresh or frozen (any variety), 8 ounces
- Garlic, 2 heads
- Ginger, fresh, 1 (1-inch) piece
- Kale, 3 bunches
- Lemons, 8
- Mushrooms, portobello, 4
- Onion, red, 1
- Onions, yellow, 7
- Oranges, 9
- Parsley, fresh, Italian, 1 bunch
- Pineapple, 1
- Raspberries, 1 pint
- Salad greens, 2 (9-ounce) bags
- Scallions, 7
- Spinach, baby, 4 (9-ounce) bags
- Strawberries, 2 pints
- Thyme, fresh, 1 bunch
- Tomatoes, cherry, 1 pint
- Tomatoes, Roma, 3
- Watermelon, 1
- Zucchini, 2

MEAT, POULTRY, AND FISH

- Chicken, rotisserie, 1 whole
- Italian sausage, chicken, 12 links
- Scallops, sea, 1 pound
- Swordfish, 2 pounds
- Turkey bacon, low-sodium, 2 ounces
- Turkey, ground, 1 pound

GRAINS

- Bread crumbs, whole-wheat, 1 container (or make from leftover whole-wheat bread)
- Couscous, whole-wheat
- Flour, all-purpose
- Flour, whole-wheat
- Hamburger buns, whole-wheat, 6
- Oat bran, 8 ounces
- Oats, old-fashioned
- Orzo, 2 (16-ounce) boxes
- Pasta, whole-wheat, 8 ounces
- Rice, brown

CANNED

- Salmon, canned, 16 ounces
- Tomato paste, 1 (6-ounce) can
- Vegetable broth, unsalted, 7 cups
- White beans, 1 (14-ounce) can

OTHER

- Almonds, 1 cup
- Apricots, dried, ¼ cup
- Brown sugar
- Capers
- Coconut, unsweetened shredded, ¼ cup
- Cranberries, dried, ¼ cup
- Dates, Medjool, 2 cups
- Olive oil, extra-virgin
- Olives, Kalamata, ½ cup
- Raisins, ¼ cup
- Walnuts, 8 ounces
- Wine, dry red
- Wine, dry white

PANTRY AND REFRIGERATOR STAPLES

(Check On-Hand Supplies)

- Allspice, ground
- Baking powder
- Baking soda
- Cayenne pepper
- Cinnamon, ground, 3 teaspoons
- Cocoa powder, unsweetened, ¼ cup
- Cumin, ground
- Garlic powder
- Ginger, ground, 3 teaspoons
- Honey, 6 tablespoons
- Italian seasoning, 2 tablespoons
- Mustard, Dijon, 1½ tablespoons
- Nutmeg, ground, 1 teaspoon
- Oregano, dried, 2 tablespoons
- Peppercorns
- Sea salt
- Tarragon, dried, 2 teaspoons
- Thyme, dried, 1 teaspoon
- Red pepper flakes
- Vinegar, balsamic, 3 tablespoons
- Vinegar, red wine, 2 cups
- Worcestershire sauce, 2 tablespoons

Menu

MONDAY

Breakfast
1 scrambled egg
2 Carrot and Bran Mini Muffins (page 93)
½ apple

Lunch
Leftover Dijon and Herb Pork Tenderloin
2 cups salad greens with 2 tablespoons
Greek Salad dressing (page 110)

Dinner
Pan-Seared Scallops with Sautéed
Spinach (page 154)
Orzo with Spinach and Feta (page 129)

Water
8 (8-ounce) glasses throughout the day

Snacks
2 to 3: mid-morning, mid-afternoon,
and evening

TUESDAY

Breakfast
1 scrambled egg
2 Carrot and Bran Mini Muffins
(page 93)
Julene's Green Juice
(3 to 4 ounces; page 86)

Lunch
White Bean Soup with Kale (page 118)
½ apple

Dinner
Baked Stuffed Portobello
Mushrooms (page 141)
Rice and Spinach (page 125)
Mixed Berry Frozen Yogurt
Bar (page 200)
3 ounces red wine

Water
8 (8-ounce) glasses throughout the day

Snacks
2 to 3: mid-morning, mid-afternoon,
and evening

WEDNESDAY

Breakfast
1 scrambled egg
Julene's Green Juice
(3 to 4 ounces; page 86)
8 ounces unsweetened nonfat plain
Greek yogurt
½ cup blueberries

Lunch
1 Carrot and Bran Mini Muffin (page 93)
Leftover White Bean Soup with Kale
½ apple

Dinner
Chicken Sausage and Peppers (page 166)
2 ounces whole-wheat pasta
Lemon and Watermelon
Granita (page 196)

Water
8 (8-ounce) glasses throughout the day

Snacks
2 to 3: mid-morning, mid-afternoon,
and evening

THURSDAY

Breakfast
1 scrambled egg
Fruit Smoothie (page 88)

Lunch
Leftover Chicken Sausage and Peppers
2 ounces whole-wheat pasta
½ cup blueberries

Dinner
Stuffed Red Bell Peppers (page 140)
Orzo with Spinach and Feta (page 129)
3 ounces dry red wine

Water
8 (8-ounce) glasses throughout the day

Snacks
2 to 3: mid-morning, mid-afternoon,
and evening

FRIDAY

Breakfast
1 scrambled egg
Leftover Fruit Smoothie

Lunch
3 cups fresh baby spinach
1 cup rotisserie chicken meat
(skin removed)
2 tablespoons Greek Salad
dressing (page 110)
½ apple

Dinner
Salmon Burgers (page 156)
1 whole-wheat hamburger bun
Balsamic Roasted Carrots (page 187)
3 ounces dry red wine

Water
8 (8-ounce) glasses throughout the day

Snacks
2 to 3: mid-morning, mid-afternoon,
and evening

SATURDAY

Breakfast
Smoked Salmon Scramble (page 96)
½ cup sliced strawberries

Lunch
Leftover Salmon Burger
1 whole-wheat hamburger bun
½ cup cherry tomatoes

Dinner
Swordfish Kebabs (page 158)
Spiced Couscous (page 126)
2 cups salad greens with 2 tablespoons
Greek Salad dressing (page 110)

Water
8 (8-ounce) glasses throughout the day

Snacks
2 to 3: mid-morning, mid-afternoon,
and evening

SUNDAY

Breakfast
Poached Eggs with Avocado
Purée (page 97)
½ orange (or 1 clementine)
2 ounces low-sodium turkey bacon
or lean Canadian bacon, crisped

Lunch
Leftover Swordfish Kebabs
Leftover Spiced Couscous
2 cups salad greens with 2 tablespoons
Greek Salad dressing (page 110)

Dinner
Moussaka (page 174)
Citrus Sautéed Spinach (page 184)

Water
8 (8-ounce) glasses throughout the day

Snacks
2 to 3: mid-morning, mid-afternoon,
and evening

SUGGESTED SNACKS
Date Nut Energy Balls, 1 (page 202)
Spiced Almonds, 1 ounce (page 102)
White Bean Dip, 2 tablespoons
(page 104) with 1 cup bell pepper slices
Part-skim mozzarella cheese stick, 1,
and ½ apple
Hummus, 2 tablespoons (page 100)

Your Personal Trainer

Your exercise plan for the week. Fill in the table with the cardio and strength-training exercises (see page 32) you plan to do.

M	T	W	TH	F	SAT	S
Cardio:	Cardio: Strength Group A: Group B: Group C: Group D:	REST	Cardio: Strength Group A: Group B: Group C: Group D:	REST	Cardio:	REST

Habit Tracker

It's important to make healthy lifestyle choices in addition to dietary changes. Keep track of healthy habits you want to maintain and mark the days when you succeed.

HABIT	M	T	W	TH	F	SAT	S

Week 3

Making changes that affect your health is a process. In Week 3, as previously, you will experiment with some foods you may have never tried before. Being healthy is best achieved by eating a variety of foods and giving your body nutrients from different food groups, so be open to the possibilities. As you continue to follow the plan this week, you may notice your skin has a new glow, you are sleeping better, and you have more energy. Get used to it—these are some of the many rewards of your new lifestyle! As you begin to feel more energized, it's a great invitation to add more reps or weight in your workouts. Remember, it's not just about what the scale says. It's also about how you feel as you become stronger and healthier.

Prep Ahead

- ◆ Hardboil or scramble 5 eggs for weekday breakfasts.

- ◆ Make Oatmeal with Berries and Sunflower Seeds (page 92) and refrigerate in single-serve portions.

- ◆ Make Cioppino (page 159) and refrigerate or freeze in single-serve containers for lunches.

- ◆ Make a batch of White Bean Soup with Kale (page 118) and freeze in single-serve containers for meals this week and next.

- ◆ Cook a batch of brown rice and freeze in single-serve (½-cup) containers.

- ◆ Make Baked Apples with Walnuts and Spices (page 197).

Shopping List

DAIRY AND EGGS

- Almond milk, unsweetened, 1 quart (can substitute skim milk)
- Butter, 1 stick (can substitute extra-virgin olive oil)
- Cheese, feta, crumbled, ½ cup
- Cheese, mozzarella, part-skim, 3-ounce block
- Cheese, mozzarella, part-skim, grated, ½ cup
- Cheese, Parmesan, grated, ½ cup
- Cheese, ricotta, 2 cups
- Eggs, 18
- Milk, skim, 1 quart
- Yogurt, Greek, unsweetened nonfat plain, 1⅛ cups

PRODUCE

- Apples, 7
- Artichoke hearts, frozen, 16 ounces
- Bananas, 2
- Basil, fresh, 2 bunches
- Bell pepper, red, 1
- Blackberries, 1 pint
- Blueberries, 1 pint
- Brussels sprouts, 1 pound
- Carrots, 1
- Carrots, baby, 1 pound
- Cauliflower, 2 heads
- Celery, 1 stalk
- Chives, fresh, 1 bunch
- Cucumber, 1
- Dill, fresh, 1 bunch
- Eggplant, 1
- Fennel bulb, 1
- Garlic, 3 heads
- Kale, 1 bunch
- Lemons, 8
- Lettuce, romaine, 3 heads
- Mushrooms, cremini, 1 pound
- Onions, red, 2
- Onions, yellow, 7
- Oranges, 4
- Oregano, fresh, 1 bunch
- Parsley, fresh, Italian, 1 bunch
- Peas, 8 ounces
- Raspberries, 2 pints
- Rosemary, fresh, 1 bunch
- Salad greens, 1 (9-ounce) bag
- Shallot, 1
- Spinach, baby, 1 (16-ounce) container
- Squash, spaghetti, 1
- Strawberries, 3 pints
- Tomatoes, cherry, 1 pint
- Tomatoes, large, 3
- Zucchini, 6

MEAT, POULTRY, AND FISH

- Beef, ground, extra-lean, ½ pound
- Chicken breasts, boneless, skinless, 4 plus 1½ pounds
- Chicken, drumsticks, 12
- Chicken, rotisserie, 1 whole
- Cod, 1 pound
- Italian sausage, chicken, 8 ounces
- Salmon, 1 pound
- Shrimp, medium, 2 pounds
- Steak, skirt, 1½ pounds

GRAINS

- Bread, whole-wheat, light, 1 loaf
- Hamburger buns, whole-wheat, 4
- Oats, old-fashioned
- Pasta, whole-wheat, 6 ounces

CANNED

- Artichoke hearts, jarred, 1 cup
- Broth, chicken, unsalted, 2 cups
- Broth, vegetable, unsalted, 6 cups
- Red pepper, roasted
- Tomatoes, chopped, 1 (14-ounce) can
- Tomatoes, crushed, 4 (14-ounce) cans
- Tomato sauce, 2 (32-ounce) cans
- White beans, 1 (14-ounce) can

OTHER

- Olives, black, 1½ cups
- Olives, green, 1 cup
- Soy sauce, low-sodium
- Sunflower seeds, ¼ cup
- Walnuts, chopped, ½ cup
- Wine, dry red
- Wine, dry white
- Yeast, quick-rising, 1 package

PANTRY AND REFRIGERATOR STAPLES

(Check On-Hand Supplies)

- Capers, ¼ cup
- Caraway seeds, ½ teaspoon
- Cinnamon, ground, 1 teaspoon
- Cocoa powder, unsweetened, 3 tablespoons
- Cornstarch, 3 tablespoons
- Flour, all-purpose, ¼ cup
- Flour, whole-wheat, 1¼ cups
- Garlic powder, 1 teaspoon
- Ginger, ground, ¼ teaspoon
- Honey, 7 tablespoons
- Italian seasoning, 5 tablespoons
- Mustard, Dijon, 3 tablespoons
- Nutmeg, ground, 1¼ teaspoons
- Olive oil, extra-virgin
- Oregano, dried, 3 tablespoons
- Peppercorns
- Red pepper flakes
- Rice, brown
- Sea salt
- Sugar, ½ cup
- Thyme, dried, 2 tablespoons
- Vanilla extract, 2 teaspoons
- Vinegar, red wine, ½ cup

MONDAY

Breakfast
1 egg, cooked your way
Oatmeal with Berries and Sunflower
Seeds (page 92)

Lunch
Leftover Moussaka
2 cups salad greens with 2 tablespoons
Greek Salad dressing (page 110)

Dinner
Spinach and Feta–Stuffed Chicken
Breasts (page 170)
Mashed Cauliflower (page 185)
½ cup cooked brown rice

Water
8 (8-ounce) glasses throughout the day

Snacks
2 to 3: mid-morning, mid-afternoon,
and evening

TUESDAY

Breakfast
1 egg, cooked your way
2 Carrot and Bran Mini Muffins
(page 93)
½ orange (or 1 clementine)

Lunch
White Bean Soup with Kale (frozen)
½ apple

Dinner
Steak with Red Wine–Mushroom
Sauce (page 176)
Greek Salad (page 110)
Baked Apples with Walnuts and
Spices (page 197)
3 ounces dry red wine

Water
8 (8-ounce) glasses throughout the day

Snacks
2 to 3: mid-morning, mid-afternoon,
and evening

WEDNESDAY

Breakfast
1 egg, cooked your way
Berry and Yogurt Parfait (page 89)

Lunch
1 Carrot and Bran Mini Muffin (page 93)
Cioppino (page 159)
½ orange (or 1 clementine)

Dinner
Shrimp Scampi (page 152)
2 ounces whole-wheat pasta
2 cups salad greens with 2 tablespoons
Greek Salad dressing (page 110)

Water
8 (8-ounce) glasses throughout the day

Snacks
2: mid-morning and mid-afternoon

THURSDAY

Breakfast
1 egg, scrambled
Chocolate Banana Smoothie (page 87)

Lunch
Leftover Cioppino
½ cup cooked brown rice
½ orange (or 1 clementine)

Dinner
Chicken Piccata (page 167)
Artichokes Aginares al Greco (page 193)

Water
8 (8-ounce) glasses throughout the day

Snacks
2 to 3: mid-morning, mid-afternoon,
and evening

FRIDAY

Breakfast
1 egg, scrambled
Leftover Chocolate Banana Smoothie

Lunch
White Bean Soup with Kale (frozen)
½ orange (or 1 clementine)

Dinner
Burger night: 3-ounce extra-lean ground
beef patty
1 whole-wheat hamburger bun
Easy Brussels Sprouts Hash (page 182)

Water
8 (8-ounce) glasses throughout the day

Snacks
2 to 3: mid-morning, mid-afternoon,
and evening

SATURDAY

Breakfast
Tomato and Zucchini Frittata (page 95)
½ cup sliced strawberries

Lunch
Chop Chop Salad (page 114)
1 Carrot and Bran Mini Muffin (page 93)
½ apple

Dinner
Easy Zucchini Lasagna Wraps (page 147)
Flatbread with Olive Tapenade (page 137)

Water
8 (8-ounce) glasses throughout the day

Snacks
2 to 3: mid-morning, mid-afternoon,
and evening

SUNDAY

Breakfast
French Toast (page 94)
½ cup sliced strawberries
1 egg, cooked your way

Lunch
Leftover Chop Chop Salad
½ apple

Dinner
Rosemary Baked Chicken
Drumsticks (page 171)
Spaghetti Squash Marinara (page 145)
Vanilla Pudding with
Strawberries (page 199)
3 ounces dry red wine

Water
8 (8-ounce) glasses throughout the day

Snacks
2 to 3: mid-morning, mid-afternoon,
and evening

SUGGESTED SNACKS
Date Nut Energy Balls, 1 (page 202)
Baba Ganoush, 2 tablespoons (page 101)
with 1 cup nonstarchy veggies
Asparagus spears wrapped in
prosciutto, 3
Sweet-and-Savory Popcorn,
1 cup (page 103)
Unsweetened nonfat plain Greek yogurt,
1 cup, with ½ cup sliced fruit of choice

Your Personal Trainer

Your exercise plan for the week. Fill in the table with the cardio and strength-training exercises (see page 32) you plan to do.

M	T	W	TH	F	SAT	S
Cardio:	Cardio: Strength Group A: Group B: Group C: Group D:	REST	Cardio: Strength Group A: Group B: Group C: Group D:	REST	Cardio:	REST

Habit Tracker

It's important to make healthy lifestyle choices in addition to dietary changes. Keep track of healthy habits you want to maintain and mark the days when you succeed.

HABIT	M	T	W	TH	F	SAT	S

Week 4

Congratulations again—the final week of your 28-day diet plan is here! By now you are most likely craving less sugar and fewer refined carbs. This week, you may be tempted by a coworker's birthday cake or a friend's invitation to go for ice cream, but remember why you started. You committed to finishing this plan, and you are one food shop and prep away from achieving that. You *will* have birthday cake again—but Week 4 is especially important because it solidifies your commitment to the plan and your dedication to eating healthy. You'll continue to try new recipes and now you can mark which ones you like the best so you can make them again. Celebrate this last week by sharing your experience with a friend or family member—invite them over to try a favorite dish or two. You will also be rounding out your 28-day trial with the "personal trainer" and continuing to use your logs to track your habits.

Prep Ahead

- Hardboil or scramble 5 eggs.
- Make Almond and Maple Quick Grits (page 91) and refrigerate to reheat for breakfasts.
- Cook brown rice and freeze in single-serve (½-cup) containers.
- Make Hummus (page 100).

Shopping List

DAIRY AND EGGS

- Almond milk, unsweetened, 1 quart (can substitute skim milk)
- Cheese, feta, 4 ounces (½ cup)
- Cheese, string, low-fat, 4
- Eggs, 20
- Yogurt, Greek, unsweetened nonfat plain, 2½ cups

PRODUCE

- Apple, 1
- Avocados, 2
- Basil, fresh, 1 bunch
- Beans, green, 1 pound
- Bell peppers, red, 3
- Blackberries, 1 pint
- Blueberries, 2 pints
- Cantaloupe, 1
- Carrots, 3
- Carrots, baby, 1 pound
- Celery, 1 stalk
- Cilantro, fresh, 1 bunch
- Cucumber, 1
- Fennel bulb, 1
- Fruit of choice, 2 cups
- Garlic, 3 heads
- Grapes, 1½ cups
- Kale, 1 bunch
- Lemons, 7
- Lettuce, romaine, 1 head
- Lime, 1
- Mint, fresh, 2 bunches
- Mushrooms, 8 ounces
- Onions, red, 2
- Onions, yellow, 4
- Oregano, fresh, 1 bunch
- Parsley, fresh, Italian, 2 bunches
- Peach, 1
- Pears, 4
- Plums, 2
- Raspberries, 1 pint
- Rosemary, fresh, 1 bunch
- Salad greens, 1 (16-ounce) container
- Scallions, 6
- Strawberries, 1 pint
- Thyme, fresh, 1 bunch
- Tomatoes, cherry, 1 pint
- Tomatoes, grape, 1 pint
- Tomatoes, large, 3
- Zucchini, 2

MEAT, POULTRY, AND FISH

- Chicken breast, boneless, skinless, 12 ounces
- Halibut, 4 (6-ounce) fillets
- Italian sausage, chicken, 1 pound
- Lamb chops, 6
- Salmon, smoked, 4 ounces
- Shrimp, medium, 1 pound
- Turkey breast, bone-in, 1 (6-pound)
- Turkey, ground, 1¼ pounds

GRAINS

- Couscous, whole-wheat
- Grits, quick-cooking
- Hamburger buns, whole-wheat, 4
- Spaghetti, whole-wheat, 8 ounces

CANNED

- Broth, chicken, unsalted, 6 cups
- Broth, vegetable, unsalted, 6 cups
- Chickpeas, 1 (14-ounce) can
- Tomatoes, chopped, 1 (14-ounce) can
- Tomatoes, crushed, 3 (14-ounce) cans
- Tomato paste, 1 (6-ounce) can
- Tuna, water-packed, 1 small (3-ounce) can
- White beans, 1 (14-ounce) can

OTHER

- Almonds, slivered, ¼ cup
- Anchovy paste
- Olives, black, 5 cups
- Olives, Kalamata, 8
- Olive oil mayonnaise
- Syrup, maple, pure
- Walnuts, ¼ cup
- Wine, dry red
- Wine, dry white
- Yogurt, frozen, low-fat vanilla

PANTRY AND REFRIGERATOR STAPLES

(Check On-Hand Supplies)

- Bread crumbs, whole-wheat, seasoned, ¼ cup
- Capers, ½ cup
- Cayenne pepper
- Cinnamon, ground, 1 teaspoon
- Ginger, ground, ½ teaspoon
- Honey, 2 tablespoons
- Italian seasoning, 1 tablespoon
- Mustard, Dijon, 1 teaspoon
- Mustard, dried, 1 teaspoon
- Olive oil, extra-virgin
- Oregano, dried, 2 tablespoons
- Peppercorns
- Red pepper flakes
- Rice, brown
- Sea salt
- Thyme, dried, 1 teaspoon
- Vinegar, red wine, ½ cup

Menu

MONDAY

Breakfast
1 egg, cooked your way
Almond and Maple Quick Grits
(page 91; precooked if desired)

Lunch
Leftover Rosemary Baked
Chicken Drumsticks
2 cups salad greens with 2 tablespoons
Greek Salad dressing (page 110)

Dinner
Shrimp Mojo de Ajo (page 153)
½ cup cooked brown rice
½ cup baby carrots

Water
8 (8-ounce) glasses throughout the day

Snacks
2: mid-morning and mid-afternoon

TUESDAY

Breakfast
1 egg, cooked your way
2 Carrot and Bran Mini Muffins
(page 93)
½ cup sliced berries

Lunch
White Bean Soup with Kale (page 118)
½ apple

Dinner
Halibut en Papillote with Capers, Onions,
Olives, and Tomatoes (page 160)
Steamed broccoli (1 to 2 cups)
Fruit Salad with Yogurt Cream (page 201)

Water
8 (8-ounce) glasses throughout the day

Snacks
2 to 3: mid-morning, mid-afternoon,
and evening

WEDNESDAY

Breakfast
1 egg, cooked your way
Leftover Almond and Maple Quick Grits
½ cup blueberries

Lunch
1 Carrot and Bran Mini Muffin (page 93)
Cioppino (frozen)
½ pear

Dinner
Lamb with String Beans (page 179)
Tabbouleh (page 128)
3 ounces dry red wine

Water
8 (8-ounce) glasses throughout the day

Snacks
2 to 3: mid-morning, mid-afternoon,
and evening

THURSDAY

Breakfast
1 egg, cooked your way
Berry and Yogurt Parfait (page 89)

Lunch
Tuna salad made with 3 ounces drained
water-packed tuna, 2 tablespoons
olive oil mayonnaise, 1 teaspoon Dijon
mustard, and 1 chopped celery stalk
2 whole-wheat bread slices
½ pear

Dinner
Herb-Roasted Turkey Breast (page 165)
2 cups salad greens with 2 tablespoons
Greek Salad dressing (page 110)

Water
8 (8-ounce) glasses throughout the day

Snacks
2: mid-morning and mid-afternoon

FRIDAY

Breakfast
1 egg, cooked your way
2 Carrot and Bran Mini Muffins
(page 93)

Lunch
White Bean Soup with Kale (page 118)
½ pear

Dinner
Burger night: 3-ounce Italian chicken
sausage patty mixed with chopped
roasted red bell pepper
1 whole-wheat hamburger bun
½ cup baby carrots
3 ounces dry red wine

Water
8 (8-ounce) glasses throughout the day

Snacks
2 to 3: mid-morning, mid-afternoon,
and evening

SATURDAY

Breakfast
Smoked Salmon Scramble (page 96)
½ pear
1 slice whole-wheat toast

Lunch
Pasta Puttanesca (page 130)
½ pear

Dinner
Greek Meatballs (page 178)
Greek Salad (page 110)
3 ounces dry red wine

Water
8 (8-ounce) glasses throughout the day

Snacks
2: mid-morning and mid-afternoon

SUNDAY

Breakfast
Poached Eggs with Avocado
Purée (page 97)
Fruit Smoothie (page 88)

Lunch
Leftover Pasta Puttanesca
Leftover Greek Salad or 2 cups salad
greens with 2 tablespoons Greek Salad
dressing (page 110)

Dinner
Chicken and Vegetable Soup (page 120)
½ cup cooked brown rice
½ cup vanilla frozen yogurt

Water
8 (8-ounce) glasses throughout the day

Snacks
2 to 3: mid-morning, mid-afternoon,
and evening

SUGGESTED SNACKS
Date Nut Energy Balls, 1 (page 202)
Carrot and Bran Mini Muffins,
1 to 2 (page 93)
Low-fat string cheese (1) with
½ apple
Spiced Almonds, 1 ounce (page 102)
Marinated Olives, ¼ cup (page 105)

Your Personal Trainer

Your exercise plan for the week. Fill in the table with the cardio and strength-training exercises (see page 32) you plan to do.

M	T	W	TH	F	SAT	S
Cardio:	Cardio: Strength Group A:	REST	Cardio: Strength Group A:	REST	Cardio:	REST
	Group B:		Group B:			
	Group C:		Group C:			
	Group D:		Group D:			

Habit Tracker

It's important to make healthy lifestyle choices in addition to dietary changes. Keep track of healthy habits you want to maintain and mark the days when you succeed.

HABIT	M	T	W	TH	F	SAT	S

5

Beyond 28 Days

Congratulations! You made it through the 28 days of diet and exercise to which you committed on Day 1. You have changed your body, mind, and health for the better—and this is just the beginning. You have set the groundwork for a lifestyle change that will help you achieve continued weight-loss and wellness goals. By now you have likely lost weight (if that is what you sought to do), have improved your health, and overall feel better physically and mentally.

Going forward, continue to embrace all the tenets that got you here—commitment, planning, goal-setting, healthy eating, exercise, rest, and mindfulness. Revisit the early chapters to remind yourself how you got here—what made it all possible. This could not be achieved without your willingness to follow through on this commitment to yourself. Don't you feel great? And when you feel great, you'll be inspired to be the best you can in all aspects of your life.

Adjusting Priorities

In the last 28 days you made a choice to work toward a healthy lifestyle—and you did it. Maintaining this shift in your mind-set will help you continue to build on the progress you've already made—the key moving forward is to prioritize yourself.

Make time physically and mentally for your goals. Pay continued attention to what you need to achieve and maintain your goals—this is critical for long-term success with health and weight loss. The more you involve yourself in the process, the easier and quicker your new lifestyle will become second nature.

Yes, finding time to food shop and prep, staying on track, and keeping motivated can pose serious challenges, especially when trying to learn new habits. Be watchful for old habits that can result in lapses in healthy eating, exercise, and self-care activities. This is where your attention is needed. Remember, you are in charge of *you*. As you make consistently good decisions, your healthy habits grow stronger roots each day, replacing those old habits pulled up by their roots—don't let them reattach!

Dieting Success

Your job now is to keep up the good habits you've developed in the first 28 days as you work toward your long-term goals. Granted, it's not always easy to get activity in, or say no to that tray of cookies at the office. There will always be something that tempts an excuse to indulge, but the more you stay mindful of your long-term goals, the more natural it will feel to simply do the right thing. Read on for tips to keep your momentum strong:

MAP AN EXERCISE PLAN. Decide how many days you can commit to and plan these days into your schedule. If you don't work on the weekend, set aside Saturday and Sunday as two of your exercise days. If you get home early on a specific day, pick that day to do your cardio. Whatever your schedule, it's more likely to get done when you have a solid plan. Record how much exercise you do in your daily log so you can track your success week after week.

OUTWIT THE CRAVINGS—LEARN THE 3 Ds! Think of cravings as back-pedalers. You worked so hard to move forward. Giving in to cravings offers a quick fix for your immediate desires, but it also sets another new habit in motion, which puts you at risk of gaining back weight or abandoning the plan.

TO PREVENT UNHEALTHY FOOD CRAVINGS: *DRINK*, *DETOUR*, AND *DISTRACT*. First, drink water. Sometimes we are just thirsty, not hungry, and a few gulps of water can reduce the appetite, giving us time to find a healthier option. Second, detour your attention to a better food choice, such as a protein. This will fill you up and keep you satisfied longer than any treat. Finally, distract yourself. Move away from that tempting situation. Leave the house, the office, wherever that temptation lurks. Go for a walk or call a friend. Grab a piece of fruit.

WORKOUTS THAT DON'T FEEL LIKE WORKOUTS

Sometimes you might not feel like doing your usual workout. Other times you may just want to have fun and try some unconventional ways to burn calories. Here are some creative workouts in disguise:

DANCE: Crank up the music and your heart rate! If you seriously get down and dance, you'll be sweating within 10 minutes. Try hip-hop and you may find yourself drenched in sweat. There's also Zumba, tango, and flamenco—check them out!

YOGA: Yoga is relaxing, and it also builds flexibility and strength. There are many kinds of yoga, so investigate different kinds to see which is best for you.

PLAY A MUSICAL INSTRUMENT: Did you know playing the violin for an hour burns about as many calories as walking for an hour? Strike a chord and move toward your fitness goals.

PLAY A CHILDHOOD GAME: Twister, dodgeball, or tag, anyone? You're "it!" Get a few friends or family members together and burn that dinner off. You'll have so much fun, too.

PLAY ACTIVE VIDEO GAMES: Many video game systems now come with interactive games such as tennis, fitness, and dance. A half hour is fun and exhausting, and keeps you off the couch.

FORGIVE (BUT DON'T FORGET) YOUR SLIP-UPS. Slip-ups will happen. Don't let them ruin your entire day—let them serve as a call to revisit your reasons for changing your lifestyle. Get back on track as soon as possible. If you had a piece of cake for dessert, don't punish yourself with a bowl of ice cream. If you had a cookie, you don't need to eat three more in despair. Because this is a plan for life, there will be times when you indulge more than you planned. This is all part of building new habits for life. When this happens and you get through it, you'll feel good knowing you are capable of getting back on track.

SHOP WITH A FULL BELLY AND A LIST. Try not to go food shopping on an empty stomach. Always bring a list and promise to stick to it so you are not tempted to buy things you don't need. If you see something you can't resist, write it down. This will help you identify patterns so you can see what your body craves and explore healthier solutions that will satisfy the same sweet, savory, or spicy urge. Now that you're on a healthy plan, it's not always necessary to go up and down the processed food aisles. Steer clear of the tempting food aisles. Remember, you control the cart—and if a food isn't in your home, you can't eat it!

BE AN INFORMED AND PREPARED DINER. When going out to eat or to parties, make your plan as much of a priority as your outfit. Eat a light lunch if you know you are going out for dinner. Choose a restaurant with a wide range of options, and consider what you will order ahead of time. If available, review the menu online. Eat a nutrient-dense snack beforehand so you don't arrive at your destination starving. Once there, avoid the infamous bread basket and focus on obtaining a salad. When you order food, don't hesitate to make special requests that support your healthy lifestyle, such as asking for proteins grilled and vegetables steamed or substitutions like a baked potato or a whole grain instead of fries. Ask for dressings and sauces on the side, and dip your food instead of pouring the dressings on. For portion control, order an appetizer instead of an entrée along with a salad, or split a meal with someone. If you get your own meal, you can always cut your portion in half and take home leftovers for the next day. If dessert is important to you, have a bite or two of something divine, or opt for fresh fruit or sorbet. Keep your hands busy with a coffee or herbal tea and your mind busy with good conversation!

NEVER LEAVE EMPTY-HANDED. Whether you're going out for the evening or for an entire workday, always leave the house with some nonperishable fruit or nuts. You want to be prepared when you need something to eat in a pinch.

Supplemental Menus

For added variety, on the following pages are two extra weekly menus you can use or borrow from as you move past your initial 28-day plan.

Week 1

MONDAY

Breakfast
2 ounces lean Canadian bacon
¼ cantaloupe
1 cup unsweetened nonfat plain
Greek yogurt

Lunch
Salmon salad sandwich made from
3 ounces canned salmon, 2 tablespoons
olive oil mayonnaise, and the zest
of 1 lemon
2 whole-wheat bread slices
½ cup baby carrots
½ apple

Dinner
8 grilled asparagus spears
3 ounces salmon, salt, pepper, 3 onion
slices, juice of ½ lemon; wrapped in
parchment and cooked at 350°F until the
salmon is opaque, 10 to 15 minutes
Vanilla Pudding with
Strawberries (page 199)

TUESDAY

Breakfast
Smoothie made from 1 cup apple juice,
1 cup fresh baby spinach, 1 banana,
1 cup almond milk, and ½ cup
crushed ice
1 egg, cooked your way

Lunch
Three-Bean Vegetable Chili (page 144)
2 cups salad greens and 2 tablespoons
Greek Salad dressing (page 110)
¼ cantaloupe

Dinner
Pizza with Arugula and Balsamic Glaze
(page 134) topped with a fried egg
Red Wine Poached Pears (page 198)

WEDNESDAY

Breakfast
Fruit Smoothie (page 88)
1 egg, cooked your way

Lunch
Leftover Three-Bean Vegetable Chili
1 cup sliced red bell pepper
½ apple

Dinner
Chicken Kapama (page 169)
2 ounces whole-wheat pasta
Greek Salad (page 110)

THURSDAY

Breakfast
Leftover Fruit Smoothie
2 ounces lean Canadian bacon

Lunch
Leftover Chicken Kapama
Leftover Greek Salad

Dinner
Zucchini and Meatball Soup (page 121)
1 slice whole-grain toast
3 ounces dry red wine

FRIDAY

Breakfast
Chocolate Banana Smoothie (page 87)
2 ounces lean Canadian bacon

Lunch
Leftover Zucchini and Meatball Soup
1 Carrot and Bran Mini Muffin (page 93)
½ pear

Dinner
Burger night: lamb burger made with
3 ounces ground lamb, 1 tablespoon
olive oil mayonnaise, arugula, and
tomatoes
1 whole-wheat hamburger bun
Parmesan Zucchini Sticks (page 188)
3 ounces dry red wine

SATURDAY

Breakfast
Scrambled egg sandwich made with
1 egg, 2 egg whites, and 2 ounces crisped
lean Canadian bacon
2 slices whole-wheat bread
½ cup sliced strawberries

Lunch
Simple Summer Gazpacho (page 116)
3 ounces skinless rotisserie chicken
½ pear

Dinner
Spanakopita (page 148)
Tourli Greek Baked Vegetables (page 192)
Baked Apples with Walnuts and
Spices (page 197)

SUNDAY

Breakfast
1 egg baked in an avocado half at
425°F for 15 minutes
½ cup strawberries

Lunch
2 cups salad greens with 1 cup rotisserie
chicken (skinless) and 2 tablespoons
Greek Salad dressing (page 110)
1 Carrot and Bran Mini Muffin (page 93)

Dinner
Chicken Gyros with Tzatziki (page 173)
½ whole-wheat pita
Balsamic Roasted Carrots (page 187)

SUGGESTED SNACKS
Sweet-and-Savory Popcorn,
1 cup (page 103)
Carrots, ½ cup, and Hummus,
2 tablespoons (page 100)
Cherry tomatoes, 10, with 2 ounces
part-skim mozzarella
White Bean Dip, 2 tablespoons
(page 104), with 1 cup sliced bell pepper
Tzatziki Sauce, 2 tablespoons (page 106),
with fresh vegetables for dipping

WEEK 1

Week 2

MONDAY

Breakfast
1 slice whole-wheat toast spread with
¼ avocado, mashed
1 egg

Lunch
Butternut Squash Soup (page 117)
1 cup rotisserie chicken, skinless

Dinner
4 ounces grilled skinless chicken breasts
Farro with Artichoke Hearts (page 124)
½ cup unsweetened applesauce

TUESDAY

Breakfast
Julene's Green Juice,
3 to 4 ounces (page 86)
1 egg, cooked your way
2 Carrot and Bran Mini Muffins
(page 93)

Lunch
Pasta with Pesto (page 131)
1 ground turkey breast patty
½ cup blueberries

Dinner
Falafel Patties (page 142) on a bed of
arugula and chopped tomatoes tossed
with 1 tablespoon extra-virgin olive oil,
the juice of 1 lemon, 1 minced garlic
clove, and ¼ teaspoon sea salt
Mixed Berry Frozen Yogurt
Bar (page 200)

WEDNESDAY

Breakfast
Berry and Yogurt Parfait (page 89)
Julene's Green Juice,
3 to 4 ounces (page 86)

Lunch
Lentil Soup (page 119)
3 ounces cooked Italian chicken sausage
½ orange (or 1 clementine)

Dinner
Cioppino (page 159)
2 ounces whole-wheat pasta
Date Nut Energy Balls, 1 (page 202)

THURSDAY

Breakfast
Chocolate Banana Smoothie (page 87)
1 egg, cooked your way

Lunch
Leftover Cioppino
2 ounces whole-wheat pasta
½ cup blueberries

Dinner
Pan-Roasted Salmon with
Gremolata (page 155)
Mashed Cauliflower (page 185)
½ cup cooked brown rice

FRIDAY

Breakfast
8 ounces unsweetened nonfat plain
Greek yogurt with 2 tablespoons honey,
2 tablespoons chopped walnuts, and
½ apple, chopped
2 Carrot and Bran Mini
Muffins (page 93)

Lunch
Leftover Cioppino
1 Carrot and Bran Mini Muffin (page 93)
½ apple

Dinner
Salmon Burgers (page 156)
1 whole-wheat hamburger bun
½ cup baby carrots
3 ounces dry red wine

SATURDAY

Breakfast
2 eggs scrambled (in 1 tablespoon extra-
virgin olive oil) with 2 scallions, ½ red
bell pepper, and 2 ounces lean Canadian
bacon, chopped
¼ honeydew melon

Lunch
Baked Gigante Beans (page 143)
2 cups salad greens with 2 tablespoons
Greek Salad dressing (page 110) and
4 cherry tomatoes
½ orange (or 1 clementine)

Dinner
Spinach and Feta–Stuffed Chicken
Breasts (page 170)
Lemon Kale with Slivered
Almonds (page 189)
Lemon and Watermelon
Granita (page 196)

SUNDAY

Breakfast
Oatmeal with Berries and Sunflower
Seeds (page 92)
1 egg, cooked your way

Lunch
Chickpea Salad (page 113)
1 cup boneless, skinless
rotisserie chicken
½ pear

Dinner
Sun-Dried Tomato and Artichoke
Pizza (page 132)
2 ounces prosciutto (crumbed on pizza)
Red Wine Poached Pears (page 198)

SUGGESTED SNACKS
Spiced Almonds, 1 ounce (page 102)
Baba Ganoush, 2 tablespoons (page 101)
with 1 cup sliced zucchini
Marinated Olives, ¼ cup (page 105)
Unsweetened nonfat plain Greek yogurt,
1 cup, with ½ cup sliced fruit of choice
Date Nut Energy Balls, 1 (page 202)

Make Your Own Weekly Menu

Now that you've experienced the recipes in this book, I invite you to venture on your own by developing your own weekly menu. Have fun with it and capitalize on some of the dishes you enjoyed best, but remember to consult the Mediterranean balanced plate (page 22) to ensure you're getting a well-balanced diet.

	BREAKFAST	LUNCH
Monday		
Tuesday		
Wednesday		
Thursday		
Friday		
Saturday		
Sunday		

SNACK	DINNER

PART 3

The Recipes

6

Breakfast

JULENE'S GREEN JUICE   86

CHOCOLATE BANANA SMOOTHIE   87

FRUIT SMOOTHIE   88

BERRY *and* **YOGURT PARFAIT**   89

YOGURT *with* **BLUEBERRIES, HONEY,** *and* **MINT**   90

ALMOND *and* **MAPLE QUICK GRITS**   91

OATMEAL *with* **BERRIES** *and* **SUNFLOWER SEEDS**   92

CARROT *and* **BRAN MINI MUFFINS**   93

FRENCH TOAST   94

TOMATO *and* **ZUCCHINI FRITTATA**   95

SMOKED SALMON SCRAMBLE   96

POACHED EGGS *with* **AVOCADO PURÉE**   97

Left: Oatmeal with Berries and Sunflower Seeds, p. 92

3 cups dark
leafy greens

1 cucumber

¼ cup fresh Italian
parsley leaves

¼ pineapple, cut
into wedges

½ green apple

½ orange

½ lemon

Pinch grated
fresh ginger

Julene's Green Juice

Serves 1 ⬩ Prep time: 5 minutes ⬩ Cook time: None

As the name implies, I created this concoction, and now I ask for it by name at my local juice bar and have fun instructing my patients to go grab themselves a Julene's Green Juice as well. It hydrates and makes the skin glow—I'm pretty certain I can't live without it.

Using a juicer, run the greens, cucumber, parsley, pineapple, apple, orange, lemon, and ginger through it, pour into a large cup, and serve.

INGREDIENT TIPS: *Add a little orange juice for sweetness. Too much ginger can cause a burning sensation in the mouth, so I recommend a piece no larger than the size of a pinky nail.*

PREPARATION TIP: *If your juicer doesn't have the ability to prep pineapple, parsley, or ginger, use a food processor or blender for prep and mix these with the remaining ingredients.*

Per Serving (about 7.5 ounces; will vary based on water content of fruits and vegetables) Calories: 108; Protein: 11g; Total Carbohydrates: 29g; Sugars: 10g; Fiber: 9g; Total Fat: 2g; Saturated Fat: 0g; Cholesterol: 0mg; Sodium: 119mg

Chocolate Banana Smoothie

Serves 2 • Prep time: 5 minutes • Cook time: None

DAIRY-FREE
GLUTEN-FREE
MEAL IN ONE
UNDER 30 MINUTES
VEGETARIAN

Smoothies are great for breakfast on the go because they are quick, fill you up, and provide lasting energy throughout the morning. You can refrigerate leftovers and reblend the next day for about 30 seconds on high speed.

In a blender, combine the bananas, almond milk, ice, cocoa powder, and honey. Blend until smooth.

INGREDIENT TIP: *Increase the anti-inflammatory properties of this recipe by adding 2 tablespoons chia seeds or flaxseed, which are rich in omega-3 fatty acids.*

SUBSTITUTION TIP: *Allergic to tree nuts? Replace the almond milk with either nonfat dairy milk or unsweetened rice milk.*

Per Serving Calories: 219; Protein: 2g; Total Carbohydrates: 57g; Sugars: 40g; Fiber: 6g; Total Fat: 2g; Saturated Fat: <1g; Cholesterol: 0mg; Sodium: 4mg

2 bananas, peeled

1 cup unsweetened almond milk, or skim milk

1 cup crushed ice

3 tablespoons unsweetened cocoa powder

3 tablespoons honey

Fruit Smoothie

DAIRY-FREE

GLUTEN-FREE

MEAL IN ONE

UNDER 30 MINUTES

VEGAN

2 cups blueberries (or any fresh or frozen fruit, cut into pieces if the fruit is large)

2 cups unsweetened almond milk

1 cup crushed ice

½ teaspoon ground ginger (or other dried ground spice such as turmeric, cinnamon, or nutmeg)

Serves 2 ◆ Prep time: 5 minutes ◆ Cook time: None

The great thing about fruit smoothies is how easy it is to customize them using-seasonal produce. Because fruit is naturally sweet, you don't need to add any additional sweetener here. If using seasonal fruits, opt for fresh. In the absence of seasonal fruits, use frozen fruits. (The nutrition information below is based on a fruit smoothie made with blueberries and ginger.)

In a blender, combine the blueberries, almond milk, ice, and ginger. Blend until smooth.

VARIATION TIP: *Some flavor combinations to try: ginger and blueberry, honeydew melon and turmeric, mango and nutmeg, or mixed berries and cinnamon. Have fun experimenting!*

Per Serving Calories: 125; Protein: 2g; Total Carbohydrates: 23g; Sugars: 14g; Fiber: 5g; Total Fat: 4g; Saturated Fat: <1g; Cholesterol: 0mg; Sodium: 181mg

Berry and Yogurt Parfait

Serves 2 • **Prep time: 5 minutes** • **Cook time: None**

You can use any berries you like here, but the raspberries and black-berries in this recipe add a nice variety of flavors, and they don't require any chopping. These parfaits are especially good in the summer when berries are in season. Feel free to substitute any chopped fresh fruit from your local farmers' market—enjoy it at the peak of ripeness.

In 2 bowls, layer the raspberries, yogurt, and blackberries. Sprinkle with the walnuts.

SUBSTITUTION TIP: *If you are allergic to dairy products or would like to make this vegan, substitute a nondairy yogurt, such as one made from coconut milk or almond milk.*

Per Serving Calories: 290; Protein: 29g; Total Carbohydrates: 27g; Sugars: 12g; Fiber: 10g; Total Fat: 10g; Saturated Fat: <1g; Cholesterol: 15mg; Sodium: 92mg

GLUTEN-FREE
MEAL IN ONE
UNDER 30 MINUTES
VEGETARIAN

1 cup raspberries

1½ cups unsweetened nonfat plain Greek yogurt

1 cup blackberries

¼ cup chopped walnuts

Yogurt with Blueberries, Honey, and Mint

Serves 2 ◆ **Prep time: 5 minutes** ◆ **Cook time: None**

2 cups unsweetened
 nonfat plain
 Greek yogurt

1 cup blueberries

3 tablespoons honey

2 tablespoons
 fresh mint
 leaves, chopped

Tangy yogurt goes perfectly with honey, blueberries, and mint. Plus, the antioxidants in the blueberries are highly nutritious, and the yogurt's protein kick-starts your day with energy.

Apportion the yogurt between 2 small bowls. Top with the blueberries, honey, and mint.

SUBSTITUTION TIP: *If you cannot consume dairy products, try plain coconut or almond milk yogurt instead.*

Per Serving Calories: 314; Protein: 15g; Total Carbohydrates: 54g; Sugars: 50g; Fiber: 2g; Total Fat: 3g; Saturated Fat: 3g; Cholesterol: 15mg; Sodium: 175mg

Almond and Maple Quick Grits

Serves 4 • Prep time: 5 minutes • Cook time: 6 minutes

DAIRY-FREE
GLUTEN-FREE
UNDER 30 MINUTES
VEGAN

1½ cups water

½ cup unsweetened
  almond milk

Pinch sea salt

½ cup quick-
  cooking grits

½ teaspoon ground
  cinnamon

¼ cup pure
  maple syrup

¼ cup slivered
  almonds

Quick grits make a fast and easy breakfast, taking only about 10 minutes from start to finish. You can replace the maple syrup with honey. Also, use any fruits you wish in place of the almonds—just add ½ cup dried fruit at the start of cooking, or stir in fresh fruit at the end.

1 In a medium saucepan over medium-high heat, heat the water, almond milk, and sea salt until it boils.

2 Stirring constantly with a wooden spoon, slowly add the grits. Continue stirring to prevent lumps and bring the mixture to a slow boil. Reduce the heat to medium-low. Simmer for 5 to 6 minutes, stirring frequently, until the water is completely absorbed.

3 Stir in the cinnamon, syrup, and almonds. Cook for 1 minute more, stirring.

MAKE IT A MEAL: *Serve these grits alongside a softboiled or poached egg and some fruit for a well-rounded meal.*

Per Serving Calories: 151; Protein: 3g; Total Carbohydrates: 28g; Sugars: 12g; Fiber: 3g; Total Fat: 4g; Saturated Fat: <1g; Cholesterol: 0mg; Sodium: 83mg

Oatmeal with Berries and Sunflower Seeds

Serves 4 ◆ Prep time: 5 minutes ◆ Cook time: 10 minutes

1¾ cups water

½ cup unsweetened almond milk

Pinch sea salt

1 cup old-fashioned oats

½ cup blueberries

½ cup raspberries

¼ cup sunflower seeds

Oatmeal is a great way to start your day. It sticks to your ribs and is warm and satisfying. This simple oatmeal topped with fruit and sunflower seeds feels good going down, and because it's high in fiber, it will keep you feeling good all morning.

1 In a medium saucepan over medium-high heat, heat the water, almond milk, and sea salt to a boil.

2 Stir in the oats. Reduce the heat to medium-low and cook, stirring occasionally, for 5 minutes. Cover, and let the oatmeal stand for 2 minutes more. Stir and serve topped with the blueberries, raspberries, and sunflower seeds.

VARIATION TIP: *Other fruits and spices work well with oatmeal, using the same measurement proportions listed in the recipe. Try strawberries, chopped apples, or chopped pears.*

Per Serving Calories: 186; Protein: 6g; Total Carbohydrates: 32g; Sugars: 4g; Fiber: 5g; Total Fat: 4g; Saturated Fat: <1g; Cholesterol: 0mg; Sodium: 96mg

Carrot and Bran Mini Muffins

Serves 18 • Prep time: 10 minutes • Cook time: 18 minutes

DAIRY-FREE
UNDER 30 MINUTES
VEGETARIAN

These fiber-ific mini muffins freeze nicely. Once they cool from baking, store them in a resealable bag in the freezer for up to six months. When you're in a hurry, grab one or two muffins for a quick meal or snack.

1. Preheat the oven to 350°F.

2. Line two mini muffin tins with paper liners, or coat with nonstick cooking spray.

3. In a large bowl, whisk the oat bran, whole-wheat and all-purpose flours, oats, brown sugar, baking soda, baking powder, cinnamon, ginger, nutmeg, and salt. Set aside.

4. In a medium bowl, whisk the almond milk, honey, egg, and olive oil.

5. Add the wet ingredients to the dry ingredients and fold until just blended. The batter will be lumpy with streaks of flour remaining.

6. Fold in the carrots and raisins.

7. Fill each muffin cup three-fourths full. Bake for 15 to 18 minutes, until a toothpick inserted in the center of a muffin comes out clean.

8. Cool on a wire rack before serving.

VARIATION TIP: *To make a dozen full-size muffins instead, adjust the baking time to 20 to 25 minutes.*

Per Serving (2 mini muffins) Calories: 115; Protein: 2g; Total Carbohydrates: 20g; Sugars: 8g; Fiber: 1g; Total Fat: 3g; Saturated Fat: <1g; Cholesterol: 14mg; Sodium: 178mg

Nonstick cooking spray

1 cup oat bran

1 cup whole-wheat flour

½ cup all-purpose flour

½ cup old-fashioned oats

3 tablespoons packed brown sugar

1 teaspoon baking soda

1 teaspoon baking powder

2 teaspoons ground cinnamon

2 teaspoons ground ginger

½ teaspoon ground nutmeg

¼ teaspoon sea salt

1¼ cups unsweetened almond milk

2 tablespoons honey

1 egg

2 tablespoons extra-virgin olive oil

1½ cups grated carrots

¼ cup raisins

French Toast

Serves 6 ✦ **Prep time: 20 minutes** ✦ **Cook time: 10 minutes**

1½ cups unsweetened
almond milk

2 eggs, beaten

2 egg whites, beaten

1 teaspoon
vanilla extract

Zest of 1 orange

Juice of 1 orange

1 teaspoon
ground nutmeg

6 light whole-wheat
bread slices

Nonstick
cooking spray

French toast is a decadent weekend morning breakfast, made even better when served with your favorite topping, such as sliced fruit. You can also refrigerate this in a resealable bag and reheat in the microwave for 30 to 60 seconds (depending on your microwave) on high.

1   In a small bowl, whisk the almond milk, eggs, egg whites, vanilla, orange zest and juice, and nutmeg.

2   Arrange the bread in a single layer in a 9-by-13-inch baking dish. Pour the milk and egg mixture over the top. Allow the bread to soak for about 10 minutes, turning once.

3   Spray a nonstick skillet with cooking spray and heat over medium-high heat. Working in batches, add the bread and cook for about 5 minutes per side until the custard sets.

MAKE IT A MEAL: *Top each piece of French toast with ½ cup sliced strawberries, and serve alongside 2 ounces turkey bacon or lean Canadian bacon that you've crisped in a nonstick pan on the stove top.*

Per Serving (1 slice) Calories: 223; Protein: 8g; Total Carbohydrates: 15g; Sugars: 6g; Fiber: 5g; Total Fat: 21g; Saturated Fat: 13g; Cholesterol: 55mg; Sodium: 126mg

Tomato and Zucchini Frittata

Serves 4 • Prep time: 10 minutes • Cook time: 18 minutes

GLUTEN-FREE

MEAL IN ONE

UNDER 30 MINUTES

VEGETARIAN

This simple frittata makes a savory, high-protein breakfast. Make it ahead of time, cut it into wedges, and refrigerate or freeze it in a resealable bag (up to four days in the refrigerator or six months in the freezer). Simply reheat in the microwave, about 60 seconds on high heat for refrigerated frittata (if it's frozen, use your thaw cycle before heating it on high heat).

1   Heat the oven's broiler to high, adjusting the oven rack to the center position.

2   In a small bowl, whisk the eggs, egg whites, almond milk, sea salt, and pepper. Set aside.

3   In a 12-inch ovenproof skillet over medium-high heat, heat the olive oil until it shimmers.

4   Add the zucchini and tomatoes and cook for 5 minutes, stirring occasionally.

5   Pour the egg mixture over the vegetables and cook for about 4 minutes without stirring until the eggs set around the edges.

6   Using a silicone spatula, pull the set eggs away from the edges of the pan. Tilt the pan in all directions to allow the unset eggs to fill the spaces along the edges. Continue to cook for about 4 minutes more without stirring until the edges set again.

7   Sprinkle the eggs with the Parmesan. Transfer the pan to the broiler. Cook for 3 to 5 minutes until the cheese melts and the eggs are puffy. Cut into wedges to serve.

3 eggs

3 egg whites

½ cup unsweetened almond milk

½ teaspoon sea salt

⅛ teaspoon freshly ground black pepper

2 tablespoons extra-virgin olive oil

1 zucchini, chopped

8 cherry tomatoes, halved

¼ cup (about 2 ounces) grated Parmesan cheese

SUBSTITUTION TIP: *If you cannot have dairy products, omit the Parmesan cheese.*

INGREDIENT TIP: *Put your unused egg yolks to good use as a skin-repairing face mask or nourishing hair moisturizer!*

Per Serving Calories: 223; Protein: 14g; Total Carbohydrates: 13g; Sugars: 8g; Fiber: 4g; Total Fat: 4g; Saturated Fat: 4g; Cholesterol: 133mg; Sodium: 476mg

Smoked Salmon Scramble

DAIRY-FREE

GLUTEN-FREE

MEAL IN ONE

UNDER 30 MINUTES

4 eggs

6 egg whites

⅛ teaspoon
freshly ground
black pepper

2 tablespoons extra-
virgin olive oil

½ red onion,
finely chopped

4 ounces smoked
salmon, flaked

2 tablespoons
capers, drained

Serves 4 ◆ Prep time: 5 minutes ◆ Cook time: 10 minutes

This is an easy make-ahead breakfast if you don't feel like cooking on a weekday morning. However, this savory dish is ready in about 15 minutes, doable even for a busy weekday.

1   In a small bowl, whisk the eggs, egg whites, and pepper. Set aside.

2   In a large nonstick skillet over medium-high heat, heat the olive oil until it shimmers.

3   Add the red onion and cook for about 3 minutes, stirring occasionally, until soft.

4   Add the salmon and capers and cook for 1 minute.

5   Add the egg mixture to the pan and cook for 3 to 5 minutes, stirring frequently, or until the eggs are set.

VARIATION TIP: *Some people find smoked salmon a wee bit salty. Substitute 4 ounces drained canned tuna, or use canned or leftover cooked salmon as a substitute for the smoked variety.*

Per Serving Calories: 189; Protein: 16g; Total Carbohydrates: 2g; Sugars: 1g; Fiber: <1g; Total Fat: 13g; Saturated Fat: 2g; Cholesterol: 170mg; Sodium: 806mg

Poached Eggs with Avocado Purée

Serves 4 • Prep time: 10 minutes • Cook time: 5 minutes

DAIRY-FREE
GLUTEN-FREE
MEAL IN ONE
UNDER 30 MINUTES
VEGETARIAN

Make quick work of this preparation by using a large nonstick skillet to poach the eggs all at once. If you'd rather poach them one at a time, use a small saucepan instead. A custard cup or ramekin can help the egg hold its shape when you drop it in the water, and the vinegar in the water helps set the proteins.

1 In a blender, combine the avocados, basil, 2 tablespoons of vinegar, the lemon juice and zest, garlic, ½ teaspoon of sea salt, pepper, and cayenne. Purée for about 1 minute until smooth.

2 Fill a 12-inch nonstick skillet about three-fourths full of water and place it over medium heat. Add the remaining tablespoon of vinegar and the remaining ½ teaspoon of sea salt. Bring the water to a simmer.

3 Carefully crack the eggs into custard cups. Holding the cups just barely above the water, carefully slip the eggs into the simmering water, one at a time. Turn off the heat and cover the skillet. Let the eggs sit for 5 minutes without agitating the pan or removing the lid.

4 Using a slotted spoon, carefully lift the eggs from the water, allowing them to drain completely. Place each egg on a plate and spoon the avocado purée over the top.

MAKE IT A MEAL: *Serve this on top of a piece of "light" whole-grain toast, and if you like, add a slice of lean Canadian bacon that you've crisped in a nonstick skillet to make a more nutritious version of eggs Benedict.*

Per Serving Calories: 213; Protein: 2g; Total Carbohydrates: 11g; Sugars: <1g; Fiber: 7g; Total Fat: 20g; Saturated Fat: 4g; Cholesterol: 0mg; Sodium: 475mg

2 avocados, peeled and pitted

¼ cup chopped fresh basil leaves

3 tablespoons red wine vinegar, divided

Juice of 1 lemon

Zest of 1 lemon

1 garlic clove, minced

1 teaspoon sea salt, divided

⅛ teaspoon freshly ground black pepper

Pinch cayenne pepper, plus more as needed

4 eggs

Snacks

HUMMUS 100

BABA GANOUSH 101

SPICED ALMONDS 102

SWEET-*and*-SAVORY POPCORN 103

WHITE BEAN DIP 104

MARINATED OLIVES 105

TZATZIKI SAUCE 106

EASY TRAIL MIX 107

Left: Baba Ganoush, p. 101

Hummus

Serves 16 • **Prep time: 10 minutes** • **Cook time: None**

1 (14-ounce) can
chickpeas, drained

3 garlic cloves,
minced

2 tablespoons tahini

2 tablespoons extra-
virgin olive oil

Juice of 1 lemon

Zest of 1 lemon

½ teaspoon sea salt

Pinch cayenne pepper

2 tablespoons
chopped fresh
Italian parsley
leaves

One of the great things about hummus is how easy it is to make variations on the traditional recipe. For example, you can add six or seven roasted garlic cloves, drained roasted red bell peppers, or chopped herbs, such as cilantro, to totally change the flavor of the blend. Serve this creamy treat with cut-up veggies, like bell peppers, celery, and carrots, or with whole-wheat pita slices.

1   In a blender, combine the chickpeas, garlic, tahini, olive oil, lemon juice and zest, sea salt and cayenne. Blend for about 60 seconds until smooth.

2   Garnish with parsley and serve.

VARIATION TIP: *To make a roasted red pepper hummus, omit the lemon zest. Finely chop 2 jarred, roasted red bell pepper slices and add them to the blender with the other ingredients. Substitute chopped, fresh basil leaves for the Italian parsley garnish.*

Per Serving (1 tablespoon) Calories: 118; Protein: 5g; Total Carbohydrates: 16g; Sugars: 3g; Fiber: 4g; Total Fat: 5g; Saturated Fat: 0g; Cholesterol: 0mg; Sodium: 67mg

Baba Ganoush

DAIRY-FREE
GLUTEN-FREE
VEGAN

Serves 6 • **Prep time: 10 minutes** • **Cook time: 15 minutes**

This is a fun and tasty eggplant dip that is easy to make ahead. It stores and travels well. In fact, you can keep it refrigerated for up to five days, so it's a perfect weekend project to portion and take along for snacks throughout the week. Spread it on whole-wheat pita slices or serve with olives or cut-up veggies, such as jicama or celery, for dipping.

1   Preheat the oven to 350°F.

2   On a baking sheet, spread the eggplant slices in an even layer. Bake for about 15 minutes until soft. Cool slightly and roughly chop the eggplant.

3   In a blender, blend the eggplant with the tahini, sea salt, lemon juice, cumin, and pepper for about 30 seconds. Transfer to a serving dish.

4   Drizzle with the olive oil and sprinkle with the sunflower seeds and parsley (if using) before serving.

VARIATION TIP: *You can also make Baba Ganoush with zucchini in place of the eggplant. Halve 4 zucchini lengthwise (no need to peel!) and cook in a 350°F oven for about 10 minutes until soft. Continue with the recipe as directed.*

Per Serving (2 tablespoons) Calories: 121; Protein: 3g; Total Carbohydrates: 7g; Sugars: 3g; Fiber: 4g; Total Fat: 10g; Saturated Fat: 1g; Cholesterol: 0mg; Sodium: 169mg

1 eggplant, peeled and sliced

¼ cup tahini

½ teaspoon sea salt

Juice of 1 lemon

¼ teaspoon ground cumin

⅛ teaspoon freshly ground black pepper

2 tablespoons extra-virgin olive oil

2 tablespoons sunflower seeds (optional)

2 tablespoons fresh Italian parsley leaves (optional)

Spiced Almonds

Serves 8 ◦ Prep time: 10 minutes ◦ Cook time: 7 minutes

2 cups raw
    unsalted almonds

1 tablespoon extra-
    virgin olive oil

1 teaspoon
    ground cumin

½ teaspoon
    garlic powder

½ teaspoon sea salt

⅛ teaspoon
    cayenne pepper

This terrific snack keeps for a week or two, tightly sealed in a container or resealable bag in the cupboard. Use raw almonds, available at most grocery stores, or specialty or health food stores, for best results.

1   In a large nonstick skillet over medium-high heat, cook the almonds for about 3 minutes, shaking the pan constantly, until the almonds become fragrant. Transfer to a bowl and set aside.

2   In the same skillet over medium-high heat, heat the olive oil until it shimmers.

3   Add the cumin, garlic powder, sea salt, and cayenne. Cook for 30 to 60 seconds, until the spices become fragrant.

4   Add the almonds to the skillet. Cook for about 3 minutes more, stirring, until the spices coat the almonds.

5   Let cool before serving.

VARIATION TIP: *Make a sweet version of this snack by coating the almonds in 1 teaspoon ground cinnamon, ¼ teaspoon ground nutmeg, ¼ teaspoon sea salt, and ½ teaspoon ground ginger as directed.*

Per Serving (¼ cup) Calories: 154; Protein: 14g; Total Carbohydrates: 5g; Sugars: 1g; Fiber: 3g; Total Fat: 14g; Saturated Fat: 1g; Cholesterol: 0mg; Sodium: 118mg

Sweet-and-Savory Popcorn

Serves 8 • Prep time: 5 minutes • Cook time: 15 minutes

DAIRY-FREE
GLUTEN-FREE
UNDER 30 MINUTES
VEGAN

Airtight storage is the key to keeping this yummy treat fresh for up to a week—it will get stale quickly if you allow any air into the resealable bag. Look for Chinese five-spice powder in the spice aisle at your local grocery store.

8 cups air-popped popcorn

2 tablespoons extra-virgin olive oil

2 tablespoons packed brown sugar

2 tablespoons Chinese five-spice powder

¼ teaspoon sea salt

1 Preheat the oven to 350°F.

2 Put the popcorn in a large bowl. Set aside.

3 In a small bowl, whisk the olive oil, brown sugar, five-spice powder, and sea salt. Pour the mixture over the popcorn, tossing to coat. Transfer to a 9-by-13-inch baking dish.

4 Bake the popcorn for 15 minutes, stirring every 5 minutes or so. Serve hot, or cool and store in resealable bags in single-serve (1-cup) batches.

VARIATION TIP: *Make a purely sweet version using the olive oil, 2 tablespoons packed brown sugar, 1 teaspoon ground cinnamon, ¼ teaspoon ground allspice, and ½ teaspoon ground ginger. Alternatively, make a purely savory version by omitting the sugar, replacing the five-spice powder with 1 teaspoon garlic powder and 1 teaspoon dried Italian seasoning, and increasing the sea salt to ½ teaspoon.*

Per Serving (1 cup) Calories: 131; Protein: 3g; Total Carbohydrates: 21g; Sugars: 2g; Fiber: 4g; Total Fat: 5g; Saturated Fat: <1g; Cholesterol: 0mg; Sodium: 61mg

White Bean Dip

DAIRY-FREE
GLUTEN-FREE
UNDER 30 MINUTES
VEGAN

1 (14-ounce) can white beans, drained

¼ cup extra-virgin olive oil

2 garlic cloves, minced

2 tablespoons chopped fresh thyme leaves

1 teaspoon Dijon mustard

Zest of 1 orange

Juice of 1 orange

½ teaspoon sea salt

Serves 8 ◆ Prep time: 5 minutes ◆ Cook time: None

Using canned white beans makes quick and easy work of this satiating dip. It's a delicious dip for sliced veggies, and it makes a tasty spread for whole-grain or nut-based crackers. Refrigerate this dip, tightly sealed, for up to five days.

In a blender or food processor, combine the beans, olive oil, garlic, thyme, mustard, orange zest and juice, and sea salt. Blend until smooth.

SUBSTITUTION TIP: *Can't find canned white beans? Substitute canned pinto or navy beans.*

Per Serving Calories: 137; Protein: 5g; Total Carbohydrates: 16g; Sugars: 3g; Fiber: 4g; Total Fat: 1g; Saturated Fat: 1g; Cholesterol: 0mg; Sodium: 128mg

Marinated Olives

Serves 8 • **Prep time: 10 minutes (plus 2 hours to marinate)** • **Cook time: None**

¼ cup extra-virgin
olive oil

¼ cup red wine
vinegar

3 garlic
cloves, minced

2 tablespoons
chopped fresh
rosemary leaves

1 tablespoon chopped
fresh thyme leaves

Zest of 1 lemon

½ teaspoon sea salt

2 cups black or green
olives, drained
and rinsed

If you like olives, this Mediterranean mainstay is a joy to the senses.
The process of marinating olives lets you add interesting flavors to
enhance their natural flavor. Buy large black or green olives that aren't
already marinated (they may be in a brine or in oil), and rinse them
well before adding them to the marinade. You can use a resealable bag
or any tightly sealed container to marinate, such as a repurposed jar
and lid that have been carefully cleaned and sanitized.

1   In a small bowl, whisk the olive oil, vinegar, garlic, rosemary, thyme,
    lemon zest, and sea salt.

2   Add the olives to your container and pour the marinade over the top.
    Seal and refrigerate for at least 2 hours. The olives will keep refriger-
    ated for up to 2 weeks.

MAKE IT A MEAL: *Include the olives as part of a festive smorgasbord with
sliced veggies, or use them as treats for dipping in Hummus (page 100) or
Baba Ganoush (page 101).*

WARNING: *Homemade garlic-infused oil carries the risk of botulism.
Consume it immediately or refrigerate for up to one week. Don't store on
the counter, and discard after a week.*

Per Serving (¼ cup) Calories: 103; Protein: 10g; Total Carbohydrates: 4g; Sugars: <1g; Fiber: 2g;
Total Fat: 10g; Saturated Fat: 2g; Cholesterol: 0mg; Sodium: 412mg

Tzatziki Sauce

Serves 8 ◆ **Prep time: 10 minutes (plus 1 hour to chill)** ◆ **Cook time: None**

1 cup unsweetened
    nonfat plain
    Greek yogurt

1 cucumber, peeled
    and grated

1 tablespoon chopped
    fresh dill

1 garlic clove, minced

¼ teaspoon sea salt

⅛ teaspoon freshly
    ground black
    pepper

This Mediterranean staple is a versatile accompaniment to many dishes, ranging from appetizers such as pita bread and fresh vegetables to chicken, fish, lamb, or pork. A chilled bowl of this sauce placed in the middle of your table is just the thing for festive family-style sharing.

In a small bowl, whisk the yogurt, cucumber, dill, garlic, sea salt, and pepper. Cover and refrigerate for 1 hour or more before serving.

SUBSTITUTION TIP: *To make this dairy free, substitute a nondairy plain yogurt, such as coconut or almond milk yogurt.*

INGREDIENT TIP: *For some reason, the garlic essence in tzatziki sauce lingers. You may want to have breath mints on hand, even the next day! A nontraditional addition that can help mitigate this is chopped fresh parsley.*

Per Serving (2 tablespoons) Calories: 29; Protein: 2g; Total Carbohydrates: 4g; Sugars: 3g; Fiber: <1g; Total Fat: <1g; Saturated Fat: 0g; Cholesterol: 2mg; Sodium: 82mg

Easy Trail Mix

Serves 8 ◆ **Prep time: 10 minutes** ◆ **Cook time: None**

Trail mix makes a great snack because it's quick to toss together and offers a nice blend of protein, carbs, and fats. This version uses dried fruits for a hint of sweetness along with nuts and dried coconut.

In a bowl, combine all ingredients. Store in ¼ cup servings in resealable bags for up to six weeks.

VARIATION TIP: *Replace the apricots and cranberries with ½ cup of dried apples.*

Per Serving Calories: 144; Protein: 4g; Total Carbohydrates: 9g; Sugars: 4g; Fiber: 2g; Total Fat: 11g; Saturated Fat: 1g; Cholesterol: 0mg; Sodium: 2mg

½ cup unsalted roasted cashews

¼ cup dried cranberries

¼ cup dried apricots

½ cup walnut halves

½ cup toasted hazelnuts

Salads *and* Soups

GREEK SALAD 110

CUCUMBER SALAD 111

CAPRESE SALAD 112

CHICKPEA SALAD 113

CHOP CHOP SALAD 114

PANZANELLA 115

SIMPLE SUMMER GAZPACHO 116

BUTTERNUT SQUASH SOUP 117

WHITE BEAN SOUP *with* **KALE** 118

LENTIL SOUP (FAKI) 119

CHICKEN *and* **VEGETABLE SOUP** 120

ZUCCHINI *and* **MEATBALL SOUP** 121

Left: Panzanella, p. 115

Greek Salad

Serves 4 ⬥ Prep time: 10 minutes ⬥ Cook time: None

FOR THE SALAD

1 head romaine
   lettuce, torn

½ cup black olives,
   pitted and chopped

1 red onion,
   thinly sliced

1 tomato, chopped

1 cucumber, chopped

½ cup crumbled
   feta cheese

FOR THE DRESSING

2 tablespoons extra-
   virgin olive oil

2 tablespoons red
   wine vinegar

Juice of 1 lemon

1 tablespoon dried
   oregano (or
   2 tablespoons
   chopped fresh
   oregano leaves)

3 garlic cloves,
   minced

½ teaspoon
   Dijon mustard

½ teaspoon sea salt

¼ teaspoon freshly
   ground black
   pepper

A small Greek salad makes a delicious side dish, and doubling the portion size translates into a delightful vegetarian main course. If you make the salad to take with you, transport the dressing in a separate container and add to the salad just before serving. This recipe serves four as a side salad. As a main course, this recipe will serve two.

TO MAKE THE SALAD

In a large bowl, mix the lettuce, olives, red onion, tomato, cucumber, and feta.

TO MAKE THE DRESSING

In a small bowl, whisk the olive oil, vinegar, lemon juice, oregano, garlic, mustard, sea salt, and pepper.

TO ASSEMBLE

Just before serving, toss the salad with the dressing.

MAKE IT A MEAL: *Add 4 chopped hardboiled eggs to make this a hearty protein-filled meal.*

Per Serving Calories: 203; Protein: 15g; Total Carbohydrates: 13g; Sugars: 5g; Fiber: 3g; Total Fat: 15g; Saturated Fat: 6g; Cholesterol: 25mg; Sodium: 716mg

Cucumber Salad

Serves 4 • **Prep time: 15 minutes** • **Cook time: None**

DAIRY-FREE
GLUTEN-FREE
UNDER 30 MINUTES
VEGAN

Cucumbers make a refreshing base for a salad. While you can simply chop the cucumbers and make the salad, spiralizing the cucumbers into spaghetti-like noodles offers a fun "twist." There's no need to peel the cucumbers, either; the peel adds vibrant color.

1 In a large bowl, mix together the cucumber, tomato, and scallions.

2 In a small bowl, whisk the olive oil, vinegar, dill, garlic, mustard, sea salt, and pepper.

3 Toss the dressing with the salad just before serving.

VARIATION TIP: *Cucumbers lend themselves nicely to various flavor profiles. To change things up, omit the tomato and add 3 more scallions. For the dressing: Whisk 2 tablespoons extra-virgin olive oil, ¼ cup apple cider vinegar, 1 tablespoon grated fresh ginger, 3 minced garlic cloves, 2 tablespoons chopped fresh cilantro leaves, ½ teaspoon sea salt, and ⅛ teaspoon freshly ground black pepper.*

Per Serving Calories: 118; Protein: 3g; Total Carbohydrates: 13g; Sugars: 6g; Fiber: 2g; Total Fat: 7g; Saturated Fat: 1g; Cholesterol: 0mg; Sodium: 258mg

4 medium cucumbers, chopped or spiralized into spaghetti noodles

1 tomato, chopped

3 scallions, white and green parts, chopped

2 tablespoons extra-virgin olive oil

¼ cup red wine vinegar

2 tablespoons chopped fresh dill

2 garlic cloves, minced

1 teaspoon Dijon mustard

½ teaspoon sea salt

¼ teaspoon freshly ground black pepper

Caprese Salad

Serves 4 • **Prep time: 15 minutes** • **Cook time: None**

3 large tomatoes,
sliced

4 ounces part-skim
mozzarella
cheese, cut into
¼-inch-thick slices

¼ cup balsamic
vinegar

2 tablespoons extra-
virgin olive oil

½ teaspoon sea salt

¼ cup loosely packed
basil leaves, torn

I was lucky enough to sample this dish where it originated, on the Italian island of Capri. This simple, layered salad is fresh and color-ful and comes together in a snap. Caprese salad is especially good in summer when fresh heirloom tomatoes and basil are abundant and in season at your local farmers' market. Celebrate its Mediterranean roots by serving this salad family-style on a platter.

1   On a pretty platter, arrange the tomatoes and cheese slices alternating and overlapping in a row.

2   Drizzle with the vinegar and olive oil.

3   Sprinkle with sea salt and basil and serve.

VARIATION TIP: *Replace the balsamic vinegar with an equal amount of freshly squeezed lemon juice or red wine vinegar.*

Per Serving Calories: 152; Protein: 8g; Total Carbohydrates: 5g; Sugars: 3g; Fiber: 1g; Total Fat: 12g; Saturated Fat: 4g; Cholesterol: 18mg; Sodium: 414mg

Chickpea Salad

Serves 6 • Prep time: 10 minutes • Cook time: None

Chickpeas are an excellent source of carbs, protein, and fiber. This salad presents classic Mediterranean flavors, and the chickpeas absorb the dressing for an explosion of flavor in every bite.

1   In a medium bowl, combine the chickpeas, red onion, and cucumbers.

2   In a small bowl, whisk the olive oil, lemon juice and zest, tahini, garlic, oregano, sea salt, and pepper.

3   Toss the dressing with the salad and serve.

SUBSTITUTION TIP: *If you don't have tahini, substitute 1 tablespoon toasted sesame seeds. The flavor will be the same, although the texture of the dressing will be slightly different.*

Per Serving Calories: 231; Protein: 12g; Total Carbohydrates: 8g; Sugars: 6g; Fiber: 7g; Total Fat: 12g; Saturated Fat: 2g; Cholesterol: 0mg; Sodium: 170mg

DAIRY-FREE
GLUTEN-FREE
UNDER 30 MINUTES
VEGAN

2 (14-ounce) cans chickpeas (3 cups), drained

½ red onion, finely chopped

2 cucumbers, finely chopped

¼ cup extra-virgin olive oil

Juice of 2 lemons

Zest of 1 lemon

1 tablespoon tahini

3 garlic cloves, minced

2 teaspoons dried oregano

½ teaspoon sea salt

¼ teaspoon freshly ground black pepper

Chop Chop Salad

Serves 6 ◆ **Prep time: 15 minutes** ◆ **Cook time: None**

2 heads romaine
 lettuce, chopped

3 cups chopped
 skinless cooked
 chicken breast

1 cup canned or
 jarred (in water)
 artichoke hearts,
 drained, rinsed,
 and chopped

2 tomatoes, chopped

2 zucchini, chopped

½ red onion,
 finely chopped

3 ounces mozzarella
 cheese, chopped

⅓ cup unsweetened
 nonfat plain
 Greek yogurt

1 tablespoon
 Dijon mustard

2 tablespoons extra-
 virgin olive oil

Zest of 1 lemon

3 garlic cloves,
 minced

2 tablespoons
 chopped fresh
 basil leaves

2 tablespoons
 chopped
 fresh chives

½ teaspoon sea salt

⅛ teaspoon
 freshly ground
 black pepper

This is a fun full-meal salad packed with tasty ingredients. Buy pre-cooked rotisserie chicken for the salad (removing the skin) to make it really quick and easy. Freeze any leftover chicken, removed from the bones and chopped, in 1-cup servings in resealable bags for use in other recipes.

1   In a large bowl, combine the lettuce, chicken, artichoke hearts, tomatoes, zucchini, red onion, and mozzarella.

2   In a small bowl, whisk the yogurt, mustard, olive oil, lemon zest, garlic, basil, chives, sea salt, and pepper.

3   Toss the dressing with the salad before serving.

SUBSTITUTION TIP: *If you prefer vinaigrette in lieu of a creamy dressing, replace the Greek yogurt with ¼ cup red wine vinegar.*

Per Serving Calories: 302; Protein: 29g; Total Carbohydrates: 14g; Sugars: 5g; Fiber: 5g; Total Fat: 15g; Saturated Fat: 4g; Cholesterol: 71mg; Sodium: 480mg

Panzanella

DAIRY-FREE
UNDER 30 MINUTES
VEGETARIAN

Serves 4 • Prep time: 15 minutes • Cook time: 8 minutes

Panzanella is a traditional bread salad. This one is loaded with fresh veggies. It does contain some bread, but since the goal is to keep starches low, it isn't as bready as a traditional panzanella. However, it's just as delicious.

1   In a large skillet over medium-high heat, heat 2 tablespoons of olive oil until it shimmers.

2   Add the bread and cook for 6 to 8 minutes, stirring occasionally, until crisp and browned. Drain and cool the bread on paper towels.

3   In a large bowl, combine the cooled bread, yellow, red, and plum tomatoes, red onion, basil, and capers.

4   In a small bowl, whisk the remaining 4 tablespoons of olive oil with the vinegar, garlic, mustard, sea salt, and pepper. Toss with the salad and serve.

COOKING TIP: *Add sliced cucumbers, if you wish for additional crunch.*

Per Serving Calories: 284; Protein: 5g; Total Carbohydrates: 21g; Sugars: 6g; Fiber: 4g; Total Fat: 22g; Saturated Fat: 3g; Cholesterol: 0mg; Sodium: 399mg

6 tablespoons extra-virgin olive oil, divided

4 whole-grain bread slices, crusts removed, cut into pieces

1 cup yellow cherry tomatoes, halved

1 cup red cherry tomatoes, halved

1 plum tomato, cut into wedges

½ red onion, very thinly sliced

¼ cup chopped fresh basil leaves

1 tablespoon capers, drained and rinsed

¼ cup red wine vinegar

2 garlic cloves, minced

½ teaspoon Dijon mustard

½ teaspoon sea salt

¼ teaspoon freshly ground black pepper

Simple Summer Gazpacho

Serves 4 ◆ **Prep time: 15 minutes (plus 1 hour to chill)** ◆ **Cook time: None**

6 tomatoes, chopped

3 garlic cloves,
    minced

2 red bell peppers,
    finely chopped

1 red onion,
    finely chopped

3 cups tomato juice

¼ cup red wine
    vinegar

¼ cup extra-virgin
    olive oil

¼ cup basil leaves,
    torn

½ teaspoon sea salt

¼ teaspoon freshly
    ground black
    pepper

Fresh in-season tomatoes create a refreshing and delicious cold soup that's the perfect starter for any meal. Feel free to add different vegetables or herbs to your gazpacho based on what's seasonally available for a robust flavor profile.

In a blender or food processor, combine the tomatoes, garlic, red bell peppers, red onion, tomato juice, vinegar, olive oil, basil, sea salt, and pepper. Pulse for 20 to 30 (1-second) pulses until blended. Chill for 1 hour before serving.

VARIATION TIP: *Spice it up by adding 1 chile pepper or a few dashes of your favorite hot sauce.*

Per Serving Calories: 209; Protein: 13g; Total Carbohydrates: 23g; Sugars: 16g; Fiber: 4g; Total Fat: 13g; Saturated Fat: 2g; Cholesterol: 0mg; Sodium: 737mg

Butternut Squash Soup

DAIRY-FREE
GLUTEN-FREE
VEGAN

Serves 4 • Prep time: 15 minutes • Cook time: 35 minutes

Enjoy this soup as a tasty meal starter or pair it with a fresh salad for a light lunch. Butternut squash is a bit starchy, so keep the serving size to ¾ cup or less to keep calories under control when you're focusing on losing weight. Read the cooking tip first for safe puréeing of hot foods.

1. In a large pot over medium-high heat, heat the olive oil until it shimmers.

2. Add the onion, carrot, and celery. Cook for 5 to 7 minutes, stirring occasionally, until the vegetables begin to brown.

3. Add the broth, squash, thyme, sea salt, and pepper. Bring to a simmer and reduce the heat to medium. Simmer for 20 to 30 minutes until the squash is soft.

4. Purée the soup using an immersion blender, food processor, or blender.

COOKING TIP: *When puréeing hot liquids in a blender or food processor, use caution—steam buildup can cause the hot liquid to force the lid off the blender or food processor, resulting in burns. To purée hot liquids, double-fold a towel and place it over the lid of the blender or food processor, carefully holding the lid in place with the towel. Every 10 seconds or so, allow the steam to escape out of the top of the appliance before replacing the cover and continuing to blend.*

Per Serving Calories: 136; Protein: 2g; Total Carbohydrates: 20g; Sugars: 7g; Fiber: 3g; Total Fat: 7g; Saturated Fat: <1g; Cholesterol: 0mg; Sodium: 273mg

2 tablespoons extra-virgin olive oil

1 onion, chopped

1 carrot, chopped

1 celery stalk, chopped

4 cups unsalted vegetable broth

3 cups chopped butternut squash

1 teaspoon dried thyme

½ teaspoon sea salt

¼ teaspoon freshly ground black pepper

White Bean Soup with Kale

Serves 6 ◆ Prep time: 15 minutes ◆ Cook time: 20 minutes

- 2 tablespoons extra-virgin olive oil
- 8 ounces Italian chicken sausage (uncooked), sliced
- 1 onion, chopped
- 1 carrot, chopped
- 1 red bell pepper, seeded and chopped
- 3 garlic cloves, minced
- 6 cups unsalted vegetable broth
- 1 (14-ounce) can white beans, drained
- 4 cups chopped kale
- 1 teaspoon dried thyme
- ½ teaspoon sea salt
- ¼ teaspoon freshly ground black pepper
- Pinch red pepper flakes

As a main course, this soup contains all the necessary goods to make it hearty and satisfying. It uses Italian chicken sausage, available at most grocery stores. This dish will keep in the freezer for up to six months, so it's a great soup for making in big batches.

1. In a large pot over medium-high heat, heat the olive oil until it shimmers.

2. Add the sausage and cook for about 5 minutes, stirring occasionally, until browned. Remove the sausage from the pot with a slotted spoon and set it aside.

3. Add the onion, carrot, and red bell pepper to the oil remaining in the pot. Cook for about 5 minutes, stirring occasionally, until the vegetables are soft.

4. Add the garlic and cook for 30 seconds, stirring constantly.

5. Stir in the broth, beans, kale, thyme, sea salt, pepper, and red pepper flakes. Bring to a simmer. Reduce the heat to low and simmer for about 5 minutes more until the kale is soft.

6. Return the sausage to the pot. Cook for 1 minute more until the sausage heats through. Serve immediately.

VARIATION TIP: *To make this vegan, omit the sausage and add 1 teaspoon Italian seasoning.*

Per Serving Calories: 281; Protein: 10g; Total Carbohydrates: 30g; Sugars: 6g; Fiber: 6g; Total Fat: 10g; Saturated Fat: 2g; Cholesterol: 27mg; Sodium: 602mg

Lentil Soup (Faki)

Serves 4 ◆ **Prep time: 10 minutes** ◆ **Cook time: 20 minutes**

DAIRY-FREE
GLUTEN-FREE
UNDER 30 MINUTES
VEGAN

When I was growing up, my mom made this vegetarian staple during the season of Lent. This hearty recipe offers great depth of flavor. It's so hearty and nutritious, I now make it myself to enjoy year-round.

1　In a large pot over medium-high heat, heat the olive oil until it shimmers.

2　Add the onions, celery, and carrots. Cook for 5 to 10 minutes, stirring occasionally, until the vegetables are soft.

3　Add the garlic and cook for 30 seconds, stirring constantly.

4　Stir in the lentils, bay leaves, broth, sea salt, pepper, and red pepper flakes. Bring to a simmer. Reduce the heat to medium-low and simmer for 10 minutes, stirring occasionally.

5　Remove and discard the bay leaves. Stir in the vinegar and serve.

VARIATION TIP: *If you use dried lentils, use 1 cup and increase the simmer time to 30 minutes.*

Per Serving Calories: 288; Protein: 14g; Total Carbohydrates: 43g; Sugars: 10g; Fiber: 17g; Total Fat: 8g; Saturated Fat: 8g; Cholesterol: 0mg; Sodium: 532mg

2 tablespoons extra-virgin olive oil

2 onions, chopped

2 celery stalks, chopped

2 carrots, chopped

4 garlic cloves, minced

1 (14-ounce) can lentils, drained

2 bay leaves

6 cups unsalted vegetable broth

1 teaspoon sea salt

¼ teaspoon freshly ground black pepper

Pinch red pepper flakes

¼ cup red wine vinegar

Chicken and Vegetable Soup

2 tablespoons extra-virgin olive oil

12 ounces boneless, skinless chicken breast, sliced

2 carrots, chopped

1 onion, chopped

1 red bell pepper, seeded and chopped

1 fennel bulb, chopped

5 garlic cloves, minced

6 cups unsalted chicken broth

1 (14-ounce) can crushed tomatoes, undrained

2 zucchini, chopped

1 tablespoon dried Italian seasoning

½ teaspoon sea salt

¼ teaspoon freshly ground black pepper

Serves 8 ◆ Prep time: 10 minutes ◆ Cook time: 20 minutes

This perfect weekday lunch is easy to make ahead and store. It will keep in the refrigerator for up to four days or in the freezer for up to six months. Make a double batch of this comfort food and separate it into portions to save time and give you easy access to meals on the go.

1   In a large pot over medium-high heat, heat the olive oil until it shimmers.

2   Add the chicken and cook for about 5 minutes, stirring occasionally, until browned. Remove the chicken from the pot with a slotted spoon and set it aside.

3   Add the carrots, onion, red bell pepper, and fennel to the oil remaining in the pot. Cook for about 5 minutes, stirring occasionally, until the vegetables are soft.

4   Add the garlic and cook for 30 seconds, stirring constantly.

5   Stir in the broth, tomatoes, zucchini, Italian seasoning, sea salt, and pepper. Bring to a boil, stirring occasionally. Reduce the heat and simmer for about 5 minutes more until the vegetables are soft.

6   Return the chicken to the pot. Cook for 1 minute more until the chicken heats through. Serve immediately.

INGREDIENT TIP: *To prepare the fennel bulb, cut off the stalks and reserve them for another use. Cut the core from the bottom of the fennel in a "V" shape and discard. Halve the fennel lengthwise and chop. The remaining stalks can be added to salads, or cooked down like an onion to add to any dish.*

Per Serving Calories: 149; Protein: 15g; Total Carbohydrates: 13g; Sugars: 6g; Fiber: 4g; Total Fat: 5g; Saturated Fat: 1g; Cholesterol: 27mg; Sodium: 370mg

Zucchini and Meatball Soup

DAIRY-FREE
GLUTEN-FREE
MEAL IN ONE

Serves 6 ◆ Prep time: 20 minutes ◆ Cook time: 25 minutes

This hearty soup features flavorful meatballs, so it's a gratifying lunch or evening meal. Make it ahead—it will keep for up to three days in the refrigerator and it freezes and reheats exceptionally well.

1　In a medium bowl, mix together the turkey, yellow onion, Italian seasoning, garlic powder, ½ teaspoon of sea salt, and ¼ teaspoon of pepper. On a plate, form the mixture into ¾-inch balls and set aside.

2　In a large pot over medium-high heat, heat the olive oil until it shimmers.

3　Add the red onion and cook for about 5 minutes, stirring occasionally, until soft.

4　Add the garlic and cook for 30 seconds, stirring constantly.

5　Stir in the broth, tomatoes, remaining ½ teaspoon of salt, and remaining ¼ teaspoon of pepper. Bring to a boil. Add the meatballs and return to a boil. Reduce the heat to medium-low. Simmer for about 15 minutes, stirring occasionally, until the meatballs are cooked through.

6　Add the zucchini and cook for about 3 minutes more, until soft.

7　Stir in the basil just before serving.

INGREDIENT TIP: *To help your meatballs keep their shape, here's a handy tip that works well for many recipes. After grating the onion, place the pieces inside of a clean kitchen towel. Over the sink, squeeze and wring the towel to remove excess water from the onion.*

Per Serving Calories: 244; Protein: 23g; Total Carbohydrates: 12g; Sugars: 6g; Fiber: 3g; Total Fat: 13g; Saturated Fat: 2g; Cholesterol: 59mg; Sodium: 340mg

12 ounces ground turkey

1 yellow onion, grated and squeezed of excess water (see tip)

1 tablespoon dried Italian seasoning

1 teaspoon garlic powder

1 teaspoon sea salt, divided

½ teaspoon freshly ground black pepper, divided

2 tablespoons extra-virgin olive oil

1 red onion, chopped

5 garlic cloves, minced

6 cups unsalted chicken broth

1 (14-ounce) can chopped tomatoes, drained

3 medium zucchini, chopped or spiralized

¼ cup chopped fresh basil leaves

Starches *and* Grains

FARRO *with* ARTICHOKE HEARTS 124

RICE *and* SPINACH 125

SPICED COUSCOUS 126

SWEET POTATO MASH 127

TABBOULEH 128

ORZO *with* SPINACH *and* FETA 129

PASTA PUTTANESCA 130

PASTA *with* PESTO 131

SUN-DRIED TOMATO *and* ARTICHOKE PIZZA 132

PIZZA *with* ARUGULA *and* BALSAMIC GLAZE 134

PIZZA *with* RED BELL PEPPERS, BASIL,
ARUGULA, *and* CARAMELIZED ONION 136

FLATBREAD *with* OLIVE TAPENADE 137

Left: Pizza with Red Bell Peppers, Basil, Arugula, and Caramelized Onion, p. 136

Farro with Artichoke Hearts

Serves 6 ◆ Prep time: 10 minutes ◆ Cook time: 40 minutes

1 cup farro

1 bay leaf

1 fresh rosemary
   sprig

1 fresh thyme sprig

2 tablespoons extra-
   virgin olive oil

1 onion, chopped

2 cups frozen
   artichoke hearts,
   thawed and
   chopped

1 tablespoon Italian
   seasoning

3 garlic cloves,
   minced

2 cups unsalted
   vegetable broth

Zest of 1 lemon

½ teaspoon sea salt

⅛ teaspoon freshly
   ground black
   pepper

¼ cup (about
   2 ounces) grated
   Parmesan cheese

Farro is a grain made from hulled wheat, such as spelt. It takes about 30 minutes to cook—you add it to a hot liquid and boil it like you would rice, but most of the cook time is inactive. Farro has a nutty flavor and lots of fiber, making it a top choice for a grain-based dish.

1   In a medium pot, combine the farro, bay leaf, rosemary, and thyme with enough water to cover it by about 2 inches. Place it on the stove top over medium-high heat and bring it to a boil. Reduce the heat to medium-low and simmer uncovered for 25 to 30 minutes, stirring occasionally, until the grain is tender. Drain any excess water and set the farro aside. Remove and discard the bay leaf, rosemary, and thyme.

2   In a large skillet over medium-high heat, heat the olive oil until it shimmers.

3   Add the onion, artichoke hearts, and Italian seasoning. Cook for about 5 minutes, stirring frequently, until the onion is soft.

4   Add the garlic and cook for 30 seconds, stirring constantly.

5   Add the broth, ½ cup at a time, and stir constantly until the liquid is absorbed before adding the next ½ cup of broth.

6   Stir in the lemon zest, sea salt, pepper, and cheese. Cook for 1 to 2 minutes more, stirring, until the cheese melts.

SUBSTITUTION TIP: *Replace the farro with 2 cups cooked brown rice and reduce the broth to 1 cup.*

Per Serving Calories: 138; Protein: 7g; Total Carbohydrates: 11g; Sugars: 2g; Fiber: 2g; Total Fat: 8g; Saturated Fat: 2g; Cholesterol: 8mg; Sodium: 522mg

Rice and Spinach

Serves 6 ◆ **Prep time: 10 minutes** ◆ **Cook time: 15 minutes**

This dish combines whole grains and leafy greens for a nutritional home run. Save time by thawing rice from your freezer (see tip), or buying cooked rice, available in the rice aisle of many grocery stores.

1   In a large skillet over medium-high heat, heat the olive oil until it shimmers.

2   Add the onion and cook for about 5 minutes, stirring occasionally, until soft.

3   Add the spinach and cook for about 2 minutes, stirring occasionally, until it wilts.

4   Add the garlic and cook for 30 seconds, stirring constantly.

5   Stir in the orange zest and juice, broth, sea salt, and pepper. Bring to a simmer.

6   Stir in the rice and cook for about 4 minutes, stirring, until the rice is heated through and the liquid is absorbed.

STORAGE TIP: *Save time by cooking the rice ahead of time and freezing it in handy 1-cup servings for up to 6 months. If you plan to freeze this dish, it's best to use freshly cooked rice, not frozen.*

MAKE IT A MEAL: *This is a great side paired with grilled chicken or the Pan-Roasted Salmon with Gremolata (page 155).*

Per Serving Calories: 188; Protein: 4g; Total Carbohydrates: 31g; Sugars: 4g; Fiber: 3g; Total Fat: 6g; Saturated Fat: <1g; Cholesterol: 0mg; Sodium: 301mg

DAIRY-FREE
GLUTEN-FREE
UNDER 30 MINUTES
VEGAN

2 tablespoons extra-virgin olive oil
1 onion, chopped
4 cups fresh baby spinach
1 garlic clove, minced
Zest of 1 orange
Juice of 1 orange
1 cup unsalted vegetable broth
½ teaspoon sea salt
⅛ teaspoon freshly ground black pepper
2 cups cooked brown rice

Spiced Couscous

Serves 6 • Prep time: 10 minutes • Cook time: 15 minutes

2 tablespoons extra-
virgin olive oil

½ onion, minced

Juice of 1 orange

Zest of 1 orange

½ teaspoon
garlic powder

½ teaspoon ground
cumin

½ teaspoon sea salt

¼ teaspoon ground
ginger

¼ teaspoon ground
allspice

¼ teaspoon ground
cinnamon

⅛ teaspoon freshly
ground black
pepper

2 cups water

1 cup whole-wheat
couscous

¼ cup dried apricots,
chopped

¼ cup dried
cranberries

Need a quick side? Couscous to the rescue! This pasta cooks in a flash because of its small size, making it perfect for a weeknight meal. The spices give this dish great depth, and the dried fruits add color, nutrition, and fiber.

1   In a medium saucepan over medium-high heat, heat the olive oil until it shimmers.

2   Add the onion and cook for about 3 minutes, stirring occasionally, until soft.

3   Add the orange juice and zest, garlic powder, cumin, sea salt, ginger, allspice, cinnamon, pepper, and water. Bring to a boil.

4   Add the couscous, apricots, and cranberries. Stir once, turn off the heat, and cover the pot. Let rest for 5 minutes, covered. Fluff with a fork.

VARIATION TIP: *Add ¼ cup pine nuts in place of the dried apricots for a little crunch.*

INGREDIENT TIP: *Couscous freezes well for up to 6 months, so you can save it in ¾-cup serving sizes in resealable bags or tightly sealed containers for a quick side dish.*

Per Serving Calories: 181; Protein: 6g; Total Carbohydrates: 30g; Sugars: 5g; Fiber: 4g; Total Fat: 6g; Saturated Fat: <1g; Cholesterol: 0mg; Sodium: 157mg

Sweet Potato Mash

Serves 6 • Prep time: 10 minutes • Cook time: 20 minutes

GLUTEN-FREE
UNDER 30 MINUTES
VEGAN

Sweet potatoes are an excellent example of "eating the rainbow." Sweet potatoes contain exponentially more vitamin A than white potatoes. They also have fewer calories. Have fun adapting the flavor profiles to fit your own tastes, and see the tip for some creative suggestions to mix up the flavors of this basic recipe.

4 sweet potatoes, peeled and cubed

¼ cup almond milk

¼ cup extra-virgin olive oil

½ teaspoon sea salt

⅛ teaspoon freshly ground black pepper

1   In a large pot over high heat, combine the sweet potatoes with enough water to cover by 2 inches. Bring the water to a boil. Reduce the heat to medium and cover the pot. Cook for 15 to 20 minutes until the potatoes are soft.

2   Drain the potatoes and return them to the dry pot off the heat. Add the almond milk, olive oil, sea salt, and pepper. With a potato masher, mash until smooth.

VARIATION TIP: *Here are some alternative flavor combos to try with your sweet potatoes:* **Roasted Garlic:** *Mash in 6 roasted garlic cloves and 2 tablespoons chopped fresh chives.* **Orange:** *Replace the almond milk with ¼ cup unsweetened nonfat plain Greek yogurt, and add the zest and juice of 1 orange and ½ teaspoon ground nutmeg.* **Pineapple:** *Drain ½ cup canned crushed pineapple and warm it on the stove top or in the microwave. Stir the warmed pineapple into the hot rinsed potatoes.*

Per Serving Calories: 243; Protein: 2g; Total Carbohydrates: 35g; Sugars: 5g; Fiber: 5g; Total Fat: 11g; Saturated Fat: 3g; Cholesterol: 0mg; Sodium: 169mg

Tabbouleh

Serves 6 • Prep time: 10 minutes • Cook time: None

Tabbouleh is a spiced dish from the Levantine—the eastern coast of the Mediterranean—made with couscous, herbs, vegetables, and spices. If you have time, let the tabbouleh sit with the vegetables and dressing for about an hour—this process will reward you with intensified flavors as the couscous soaks them in.

2 cups cooked whole-wheat couscous, cooled completely (see tip)

12 cherry tomatoes, quartered

6 scallions, white and green parts, minced

1 cucumber, peeled and chopped

½ cup fresh Italian parsley leaves, chopped

½ cup fresh mint leaves, chopped

Juice of 2 lemons

¼ cup extra-virgin olive oil

½ teaspoon sea salt

¼ teaspoon freshly ground black pepper

1   In a large bowl, combine the couscous, tomatoes, scallions, cucumber, parsley, and mint. Set aside.

2   In a small bowl, whisk the lemon juice, olive oil, sea salt, and pepper. Toss with the couscous mixture. Let sit for 1 hour before serving.

COOKING TIP: *To make 2 cups cooked couscous: In a saucepan over high heat, bring 2 cups water or unsalted vegetable broth to a boil. Add 1 cup couscous, stir, turn off the heat, and cover the pot. After 5 minutes, uncover and fluff with a fork.*

Per Serving Calories: 254; Protein: 8g; Total Carbohydrates: 38g; Sugars: 9g; Fiber: 7g; Total Fat: 10g; Saturated Fat: 2g; Cholesterol: 0mg; Sodium: 181mg

Orzo with Spinach and Feta

Serves 6 • Prep time: 25 minutes • Cook time: None

This classic dish combines tiny orzo pasta with tender spinach
and slightly salty feta for a light lunch or dinner. The vinaigrette
and scallions create the harmony for a truly delightful dish.

1   In a large bowl, combine the spinach, scallions, and cooled orzo.

2   Sprinkle with the feta and olives.

3   In a small bowl, whisk the vinegar, olive oil, and lemon juice. Season
    with sea salt and pepper.

4   Add the dressing to the salad and gently toss to combine. Refrigerate
    until serving.

Per Serving (¾ cup) Calories: 255; Protein: 8g; Total Carbohydrates: 38g; Sugars: 3g; Fiber: 2g;
Total Fat: 8g; Saturated Fat: 2g; Cholesterol: 5mg; Sodium: 279mg

6 cups fresh baby
    spinach, chopped

¼ cup scallions,
    white and green
    parts, chopped

1 (16-ounce) package
    orzo pasta,
    cooked according
    to package
    directions,
    rinsed, drained,
    and cooled

¾ cup crumbled
    feta cheese

¼ cup halved
    Kalamata olives

½ cup red
    wine vinegar

¼ cup extra-virgin
    olive oil

1½ teaspoons
    freshly squeezed
    lemon juice

Sea salt

Freshly ground
    black pepper

Pasta Puttanesca

2 tablespoons extra-
virgin olive oil

6 garlic cloves,
finely minced (or
put through a
garlic press)

2 teaspoons anchovy
paste

¼ teaspoon red
pepper flakes,
plus more as
needed

20 black olives,
pitted and
chopped

3 tablespoons
capers, drained
and rinsed

¼ teaspoon sea salt

¼ teaspoon freshly
ground black
pepper

2 (14-ounce) cans
crushed tomatoes,
undrained

1 (14-ounce)
can chopped
tomatoes, drained

¼ cup chopped fresh
basil leaves

8 ounces whole-
wheat spaghetti,
cooked according
to package
instructions
and drained

Serves 4 ✦ **Prep time: 10 minutes** ✦ **Cook time: 10 minutes**

Puttanesca is a briny and flavorful pasta sauce made with olives,
capers, and tomatoes. Adjust the heat of the dish by varying the
amount of red pepper flakes you add. If you are making this for
a meal on the go, carry the sauce and pasta separately and combine
them just before serving.

1   In a sauté pan or skillet over medium heat, stir together the olive oil,
garlic, anchovy paste, and red pepper flakes. Cook for about 2 minutes,
stirring, until the mixture is very fragrant.

2   Add the olives, capers, sea salt, and pepper.

3   In a blender, purée the crushed and chopped tomatoes and add to the
pan. Cook for about 5 minutes, stirring occasionally, until the mixture
simmers.

4   Stir in the basil and cooked pasta. Toss to coat the pasta with the sauce
and serve.

VARIATION TIP: *This thick sauce works well with pasta shapes that allow
it to coat the pasta. Instead of spaghetti, try rotini, fettuccine, or farfalle
(bow tie) pasta. Use gluten-free pasta if gluten is an issue for you.*

Per Serving Calories: 278; Protein: 10g; Total Carbohydrates: 40g; Sugars: 16g; Fiber: 12g; Total Fat: 13g;
Saturated Fat: 1g; Cholesterol: 9mg; Sodium: 1,099mg

Pasta with Pesto

Serves 4 • Prep time: 10 minutes • Cook time: None

Pesto is fabulous on pasta, but it's also delicious as a topping for grilled chicken, beef, or fish. Check out the tip for ideas to change up the flavors. Pesto is best fresh—it doesn't keep well, so I recommend making it fresh and using it right away.

1   In a blender or food processor, combine the olive oil, garlic, basil, cheese, and pine nuts. Pulse for 10 to 20 (1-second) pulses until everything is chopped and blended.

2   Toss with the hot pasta and serve.

VARIATION TIP: *Using the basic proportions in the recipe, you can mix various flavors to change up your pesto. For instance, try 3 tablespoons extra-virgin olive oil, 3 garlic cloves, ¼ cup fresh basil leaves, ¼ cup fresh baby spinach, ¼ cup Asiago cheese, and ¼ cup walnuts.*

Per Serving Calories: 405; Protein: 13g; Total Carbohydrates: 44g; Sugars: 2g; Fiber: 5g; Total Fat: 21g; Saturated Fat: 4g; Cholesterol: 10mg; Sodium: 141mg

3 tablespoons extra-virgin olive oil

3 garlic cloves, finely minced

½ cup fresh basil leaves

¼ cup (about 2 ounces) grated Parmesan cheese

¼ cup pine nuts

8 ounces whole-wheat pasta, cooked according to package instructions and drained

Sun-Dried Tomato and Artichoke Pizza

Serves 6 ◆ Prep time: 30 minutes ◆ Cook time: 25 minutes

Pizza doesn't always have to be the heavy, gooey concoction you find at your local pizza place. You can make a light pizza that's equally delicious and fragrant, allowing you to enjoy the pizza without all the calories.

FOR THE CRUST

¾ cup whole-wheat flour, plus more for flouring the work surface

¾ cup all-purpose flour

1 package quick-rising yeast

¾ teaspoon sea salt

⅔ cup hot water (120°F to 125°F)

2 tablespoons extra-virgin olive oil

¼ teaspoon honey

Nonstick cooking spray

FOR THE SAUCE

2 tablespoons extra-virgin olive oil

½ onion, minced

3 garlic cloves, minced

1 (14-ounce) can crushed tomatoes

1 tablespoon dried oregano

FOR THE PIZZA

1 cup oil-packed sun-dried tomatoes, rinsed

2 cups frozen artichoke hearts

¼ cup (about 2 ounces) grated Asiago cheese

TO MAKE THE CRUST

1   In a medium bowl, whisk the whole-wheat and all-purpose flours, yeast, and salt.

2   In a small bowl, whisk the hot water, olive oil, and honey.

3   Mix the liquids into the flour mixture and stir until sticky ball forms.

4   Turn the dough out onto a floured surface and knead for 5 minutes.

5   Coat a sheet of plastic wrap with cooking spray and cover the dough. Let rest for 10 minutes.

6   Roll the dough into a 13-inch circle.

TO MAKE THE SAUCE

1   In a saucepan over medium-high heat, heat the olive oil until it shimmers.

2   Add the onion and cook for 5 minutes, stirring occasionally.

3   Add the garlic and cook for 30 seconds, stirring constantly.

4   Stir in the tomatoes and oregano. Bring to a simmer. Reduce the heat to medium-low and simmer for 5 minutes more.

TO MAKE THE PIZZA

1   Preheat the oven to 500°F (or the hottest setting).

2   If you have a pizza stone, place it in the oven as it preheats.

3   In a thin layer, spread the sauce over the rolled dough.

4   Top the sauce with the artichoke hearts and sun-dried tomatoes. Sprinkle the cheese lightly over the top.

5   Place the pizza on the stone (or directly on the rack) and bake for 10 to 15 minutes until the crust is golden.

COOKING TIP: *If you have a food processor or stand mixer, use it to make the crust and save yourself a lot of time and elbow grease. Add the dry ingredients, mix with the food processor or mixer, and with the mixer running, slowly add the wet ingredients until a sticky ball forms. In a food processor, process on high speed for 1 minute to knead. In a stand mixer, use the dough hook on high speed for 5 minutes to knead.*

Per Serving Calories: 318; Protein: 12g; Total Carbohydrates: 39g; Sugars: 5g; Fiber: 6g; Total Fat: 14g; Saturated Fat: 3g; Cholesterol: 7mg; Sodium: 524mg

Pizza with Arugula and Balsamic Glaze

Serves 6 ◆ Prep time: 30 minutes ◆ Cook time: 20 minutes

FOR THE CRUST

¾ cup whole-wheat flour, plus more for flouring the work surface

¾ cup all-purpose flour

1 package quick-rising yeast

¾ teaspoon sea salt

⅔ cup hot water (120° to 125°F)

2 tablespoons extra-virgin olive oil

¼ teaspoon honey

Nonstick cooking spray

FOR THE GLAZE

½ cup balsamic vinegar

2 tablespoons honey

FOR THE PIZZA

4 cups arugula

2 tablespoons extra-virgin olive oil

½ teaspoon sea salt

⅛ teaspoon freshly ground black pepper

For this light, fresh take on pizza, bake the crust and top it with fresh arugula drizzled with a balsamic glaze. It makes a great starter or main course. If you're making it to go, keep the baked crust separate from the glaze and arugula and assemble just before you eat it.

TO MAKE THE CRUST

1   In a medium bowl, whisk the whole-wheat and all-purpose flours, yeast, and sea salt.

2   In a small bowl, whisk the hot water, olive oil, and honey.

3   Mix the liquids into the flour mixture and stir until a sticky ball forms.

4   Turn the dough out onto a floured surface and knead for 5 minutes.

5   Coat a sheet of plastic wrap with cooking spray and cover the dough. Let rest for 10 minutes.

6   Roll the dough into a 13-inch circle.

TO MAKE THE GLAZE

In a small saucepan over medium-high heat, stir together the vinegar and honey. Simmer for about 5 minutes, stirring occasionally, until syrupy.

TO MAKE THE PIZZA

1 Preheat the oven to 500°F (or the hottest setting).

2 If you have a pizza stone, place it in the oven as it preheats.

3 Place the pizza crust on the stone (or directly on the rack) and bake for 10 to 15 minutes, until the crust is golden.

4 In a medium bowl, toss the arugula with the olive oil, sea salt, and pepper. Spread the mixture over the warm crust and drizzle with the balsamic glaze.

COOKING TIP: *Make the dough ahead of time and refrigerate or freeze it, uncooked. Wrap the dough tightly in oiled plastic wrap to refrigerate (for up to 1 day) or freeze (for up to 3 months). Thaw frozen dough in the refrigerator overnight, and allow the cold dough to stand at room temperature for 30 minutes before using.*

Per Serving Calories: 237; Protein: 5g; Total Carbohydrates: 32g; Sugars: 6g; Fiber: 2g; Total Fat: 10g; Saturated Fat: 1g; Cholesterol: 0mg; Sodium: 398mg

Pizza with Red Bell Peppers, Basil, Arugula, and Caramelized Onion

Serves 6 ◆ Prep time: 30 minutes ◆ Cook time: 1 hour

This pizza features fresh, delicious veggies with just enough cheese and savory caramelized onion. The result is fresh, flavorful, and really, really good.

FOR THE CRUST

¾ cup whole-wheat flour, plus more for flouring the work surface

¾ cup all-purpose flour

1 package quick-rising yeast

¾ teaspoon sea salt

⅔ cup hot water (120° to 125°F)

2 tablespoons extra-virgin olive oil

¼ teaspoon honey

Nonstick cooking spray

FOR THE CARAMELIZED ONION

2 tablespoons extra-virgin olive oil

1 onion, thinly sliced

½ teaspoon sea salt

FOR THE PIZZA

2 tablespoons extra-virgin olive oil

½ red bell pepper, sliced

½ cup grated mozzarella cheese

1 cup arugula

¼ cup chopped fresh basil leaves

¼ cup shaved Asiago cheese

TO MAKE THE CRUST

1. In a medium bowl, whisk the whole-wheat and all-purpose flours, yeast, and salt.

2. In a small bowl, whisk the hot water, olive oil, and honey.

3. Mix the liquids into the flour mixture and stir until a sticky ball forms.

4. Turn the dough out onto a floured surface and knead for 5 minutes.

5. Coat a sheet of plastic wrap with cooking spray and cover the dough. Let rest for 10 minutes.

6. Roll the dough into a 13-inch circle.

TO MAKE THE CARAMELIZED ONION

1. In a large skillet over medium heat, heat the olive oil.

2. Add the onion and salt. Cook for 3 minutes, stirring occasionally. Reduce the heat to medium-low. Cook for 20 to 35 minutes, stirring occasionally, until the onion is browned and caramelized.

TO MAKE THE PIZZA

1. Preheat the oven to 500°F (or the hottest setting).

2. If you have a pizza stone, place it in the oven as it preheats.

3. Brush the crust with olive oil. Spread the onion over the crust and top with the red bell pepper and mozzarella cheese.

4. Place the pizza on the stone (or directly on the rack) and bake for 15 to 20 minutes until the crust is browned.

5. Remove from the oven. Top with the arugula, basil, and Asiago cheese.

Per Serving Calories: 330; Protein: 12g; Total Carbohydrates: 28g; Sugars: 2g; Fiber: 1g; Total Fat: 20g; Saturated Fat: 5g; Cholesterol: 17mg; Sodium: 594mg

Flatbread with Olive Tapenade

DAIRY-FREE
MEAL IN ONE
VEGETARIAN

Serves 6 ◆ Prep time: 30 minutes (plus 1 hour to rise) ◆ Cook time: 5 minutes

Flatbread is similar to pizza crust, but with a heartier chew. This version bakes alone and is served with a flavorful olive tapenade for a delicious side dish, snack, or appetizer. Prepare the tapenade while the flatbread rises.

TO MAKE THE FLATBREAD

1 In a small bowl, whisk the water, honey, and yeast. Let stand for about 5 minutes, covered with a clean kitchen towel, until the yeast foams.

2 In a large bowl, whisk the whole-wheat and all-purpose flours and sea salt. Add the yeast mixture and stir until a ball forms.

3 Turn the dough out onto a floured surface and knead for about 5 minutes until smooth.

4 Brush a bowl with olive oil. Add the dough and turn to coat with the oil. Cover and place in a warm spot to rise for about 1 hour until doubled.

5 Preheat the oven to 450°F.

6 If you have a pizza stone, place it in the oven as it preheats.

7 Split the dough into 6 portions. Roll each into a thin oblong shape, ¼ to ½ inch thick. Bake the flatbreads on the pizza stone (or directly on the rack) for about 5 minutes until browned.

TO MAKE THE TAPENADE

In a food processor or blender, combine the black and green olives, roasted pepper, capers, garlic, basil, oregano, and olive oil. Process for 10 to 20 (1-second) pulses until coarsely chopped.

INGREDIENT TIP: *Make the tapenade ahead of time and store, tightly sealed, in the refrigerator for up to 1 week. The cooked flatbread will keep, tightly sealed, for up to 4 days.*

Per Serving Calories: 234; Protein: 5g; Total Carbohydrates: 25g; Sugars: 4g; Fiber: 4g; Total Fat: 14g; Saturated Fat: 14g; Cholesterol: 0mg; Sodium: 593mg

FOR THE FLATBREAD

¾ cup warm water (120°F to 125°F)

1 tablespoon honey

1 package quick-rising yeast

¾ cup whole-wheat flour, plus more for dusting the work surface

¼ cup all-purpose flour

½ teaspoon sea salt

1 tablespoon extra-virgin olive oil

FOR THE TAPENADE

1 cup black olives, pitted and chopped

1 cup green olives, pitted and chopped

2 roasted red pepper slices, chopped

1 tablespoon capers, drained and rinsed

1 garlic clove, minced

1 tablespoon chopped fresh basil leaves

1 tablespoon chopped fresh oregano leaves

¼ cup extra-virgin olive oil

10

Beans, Legumes, *and* Vegetable Mains

STUFFED RED BELL PEPPERS 140

BAKED STUFFED PORTOBELLO MUSHROOMS 141

FALAFEL PATTIES 142

BAKED GIGANTE BEANS 143

THREE-BEAN VEGETABLE CHILI 144

SPAGHETTI SQUASH MARINARA 145

ZUCCHINI NOODLES *with* **PEAS** *and* **MINT** 146

EASY ZUCCHINI LASAGNA WRAPS 147

SPANAKOPITA 148

Left: Falafel Patties, p. 142

Stuffed Red Bell Peppers

Serves 4 ◆ Prep time: 20 minutes ◆ Cook time: 50 minutes

4 red bell peppers,
tops, seeds and
ribs removed

2 tablespoons extra-
virgin olive oil

1 onion, finely
chopped

1 zucchini, chopped

3 garlic cloves,
minced

3 Roma tomatoes,
chopped

4 cups fresh baby
spinach

1 teaspoon
dried oregano

½ teaspoon sea salt

¼ teaspoon freshly
ground black
pepper

1 cup cooked
brown rice

4 ounces crumbled
feta cheese

This recipe calls for red bell peppers, but you can use any color you prefer, such as yellow, brown, orange, or green. Since they're meatless, you can make and stuff the peppers ahead and refrigerate before baking. They'll keep refrigerated, tightly sealed, for up to four days.

1   Preheat the oven to 350°F.

2   Place the peppers, cut-side up, in a 9-inch-square baking pan.

3   In a large skillet over medium-high heat, heat the olive oil until it shimmers.

4   Add the onion and zucchini. Cook for about 5 minutes, stirring occasionally, until the vegetables are soft.

5   Add the garlic and cook for 30 seconds, stirring constantly.

6   Add the tomatoes, spinach, oregano, sea salt, and pepper. Cook for about 3 minutes, stirring occasionally, until the spinach wilts. Remove the pan from the heat.

7   Stir in the rice until well blended. Spoon the rice mixture into the bell peppers. Sprinkle the feta over the tops. Add about ¼ cup water to the baking pan and cover it with aluminum foil. Bake for 30 minutes. Uncover and bake for about 10 minutes more until the cheese bubbles and browns.

SUBSTITUTION TIP: *To make this dairy free, eliminate the feta cheese and replace it with 4 ounces of your favorite shredded nondairy cheese.*

Per Serving Calories: 306; Protein: 10g; Total Carbohydrates: 38g; Sugars: 12g; Fiber: 6g; Total Fat: 14g; Saturated Fat: 5g; Cholesterol: 25mg; Sodium: 589mg

Baked Stuffed Portobello Mushrooms

GLUTEN-FREE

MEAL IN ONE

VEGETARIAN

Serves 4 • Prep time: 20 minutes • Cook time: 45 minutes

Portobello mushrooms are so large and filling, they make an excellent meatless meal. Serve alongside a starch, such as the Sweet Potato Mash (page 127), if you want an even heartier meal. Mushrooms don't keep well, so it's best to purchase and make them the same day you plan to eat them.

1 Preheat the oven to 350°F.

2 Place the mushrooms, gill-side up, on a rimmed baking sheet.

3 In a large skillet over medium-high heat, heat the olive oil until it shimmers.

4 Add the onion, zucchini, red bell pepper, kale, sea salt, pepper, and red pepper flakes. Cook for about 5 minutes, stirring occasionally, until the vegetables are soft.

5 Add the garlic and cook for 30 seconds, stirring constantly. Remove the pan from the heat.

6 Stir in the basil. Spoon the vegetable mixture into the mushroom caps.

7 Sprinkle the cheese over the tops. Bake for 30 to 40 minutes until the cheese is brown and bubbly and the mushrooms are soft.

COOKING TIP: *Clean the surface of the mushrooms by wiping with a paper towel. Use the side of a teaspoon to remove and discard the gills from the underside of the mushrooms.*

Per Serving Calories: 202; Protein: 12g; Total Carbohydrates: 15g; Sugars: 4g; Fiber: 3g; Total Fat: 12g; Saturated Fat: 4g; Cholesterol: 18mg; Sodium: 431mg

4 portobello mushrooms, stems and gills removed (see tip)

2 tablespoons extra-virgin olive oil

1 onion, finely chopped

1 zucchini, chopped

1 red bell pepper, chopped

2 cups kale

½ teaspoon sea salt

¼ teaspoon freshly ground black pepper

⅛ teaspoon red pepper flakes

4 garlic cloves, minced

¼ cup chopped fresh basil leaves

4 ounces grated part-skim mozzarella

Falafel Patties

Serves 8 ◆ Prep time: 15 minutes (plus 24 hours to rest) ◆ Cook time: 30 minutes

Falafel patties are uniquely delicious on a burger bun, or you can serve them atop a salad or garnish them in a variety of ways. Made with chickpeas and fragrant herbs and spices, these are likely to become one of your Mediterranean favorites.

1 cup dried chickpeas

1 red onion,
 minced, divided

2 tablespoons
 chopped fresh
 cilantro leaves

4 garlic cloves,
 minced

1 teaspoon dried
 cumin

1 tablespoon
 freshly squeezed
 lemon juice

1 teaspoon sea salt

1 teaspoon baking
 powder

3 tablespoons extra-
 virgin olive oil

1 tomato, chopped

¼ cup chopped fresh
 Italian parsley
 leaves

1   In a large bowl, combine the chickpeas with enough water to cover. Cover the bowl and let sit at room temperature for 24 hours to soak. Add more water as needed to keep the chickpeas covered. Drain thoroughly.

2   Preheat the oven to 375°F.

3   Line a baking sheet with parchment paper or aluminum foil.

4   In a food processor, combine the chickpeas, all but 2 tablespoons of the red onion, the cilantro, garlic, cumin, lemon juice, sea salt, and baking powder. Pulse for 10 to 20 (1-second) pulses until the ingredients are finely chopped but not puréed. Form the mixture into 8 patties.

5   Brush the patties with olive oil on both sides and place them on the prepared sheet. Bake for 10 to 15 minutes, flip, and bake for 10 to 15 minutes more until each side is golden brown.

6   Garnish with the reserved 2 tablespoons of red onion, the tomato, and parsley.

INGREDIENT TIP: *The chickpeas will triple in volume when you soak them. You can use canned chickpeas (which don't need soaking), but the patties may not hold together as well. If you choose to use canned, increase the amount to 3 cups drained canned chickpeas.*

Per Serving Calories: 148; Protein: 5g; Total Carbohydrates: 18g; Sugars: 4g; Fiber: 5g; Total Fat: 7g; Saturated Fat: <1g; Cholesterol: 0mg; Sodium: 244mg

Baked Gigante Beans

DAIRY-FREE
GLUTEN-FREE
VEGETARIAN

Serves 6 • Prep time: 10 minutes (plus overnight to soak) • Cook time: 4½ hours

My mom and grandma used to make this traditional Lenten bean dish, but today it's a staple as more people are staying away from meats. I love these beans so much, I once brought bags and bags of them home from Greece, thinking I couldn't get them in the United States. Wasn't I surprised to come back and find them on the shelves in my local Greek market!

1 Place the beans in a large bowl and cover with water. Let soak overnight. Drain the beans.

2 In a large pot over medium-high, combine the beans and the broth. Bring to a simmer, reduce the heat to low, and continue simmering for 2 to 3 hours until the beans are tender, stirring occasionally. Add additional broth or water as needed to keep the beans submerged. Once tender, drain the beans.

3 Preheat the oven to 350°F.

4 In a large pot over medium-high heat, heat the olive oil until it shimmers.

5 Add the onions and carrots. Cook for 6 to 7 minutes, stirring occasionally, until the vegetables are soft and browned. Remove from the heat and stir in the beans, tomatoes, vinegar, pepper, and dill. Transfer the mixture to an 8-by-11-inch baking dish and bake for 1 hour.

6 If the sauce is runny, transfer the mixture to a pan, place it on the stove top over low heat, and bring it to a simmer. Cook for 10 to 15 minutes more until the sauce reduces. Taste and adjust the seasonings as desired, adding sea salt and more pepper if needed.

SUBSTITUTION TIP: *If you can't find gigante beans, substitute dried white northern or cannellini beans. To save time, use canned cannellini beans. If you use canned beans, omit the chicken broth and don't preboil the beans.*

INGREDIENT TIP: *While this dish might tempt you to take more than 1 serving, too much of a good thing (beans) can result in digestive discomfort.*

Per Serving Calories: 376; Protein: 29g; Total Carbohydrates: 39g; Sugars: 5g; Fiber: 7g; Total Fat: 10g; Saturated Fat: 1g; Cholesterol: 0mg; Sodium: 876mg

1 pound dried gigante beans

8 cups unsalted chicken broth, plus more as needed

¼ cup extra-virgin olive oil

2 onions, chopped

2 carrots, chopped

3 garlic cloves, minced

1 (28-ounce) can whole plum tomatoes in juice, chopped

¼ cup red wine vinegar

½ teaspoon freshly ground black pepper, plus more as needed

1 cup chopped fresh dill

Sea salt

Three-Bean Vegetable Chili

Serves 8 • Prep time: 20 minutes • Cook time: 20 minutes

2 tablespoons extra-virgin olive oil

2 green bell peppers, seeded and chopped

1 onion, chopped

6 garlic cloves, minced

1 (14-ounce) can kidney beans, drained

1 (14-ounce) can black beans, drained

1 (14-ounce) can pinto beans, drained

2 (14-ounce) cans crushed tomatoes

1 tablespoon chili powder

1 teaspoon ground cumin

1 teaspoon sea salt

¼ teaspoon cayenne pepper

Chili is always a great option for cool fall and winter evenings. It also keeps well—just freeze it in 1-cup servings and thaw as needed. Substitute any beans you like for those called for in this recipe.

1   In a large pot over medium-high heat, heat the olive oil until it shimmers.

2   Add the green bell peppers and onion. Cook for about 5 minutes, stirring occasionally, until soft.

3   Add the garlic and cook for 30 seconds, stirring constantly.

4   Stir in the kidney beans, black beans, pinto beans, tomatoes, chili powder, cumin, sea salt, and cayenne. Bring to a simmer. Reduce the heat to medium-low and cook for 10 minutes more, stirring occasionally. Remove from the heat and serve.

VARIATION TIP: *Two unexpected ingredients will enrich the flavor of your chili: Add 2 tablespoons unsweetened cocoa powder and ¼ cup bourbon along with the tomatoes.*

Per Serving Calories: 343; Protein: 19g; Total Carbohydrates: 58g; Sugars: 9g; Fiber: 16g; Total Fat: 5g; Saturated Fat: <1g; Cholesterol: 0mg; Sodium: 443mg

Spaghetti Squash Marinara

Serves 4 • **Prep time: 20 minutes** • **Cook time: 45 minutes**

While spaghetti squash takes a while to cook, it's inactive time, and the marinara sauce comes together in less than 20 minutes while the squash bakes. There's even a slow cooker option for the squash (see tip), so you can leave the squash to cook throughout the day, and all you'll need to do is make the marinara!

1 Preheat the oven to 375°F.

2 Place the squash, cut-side down, on a rimmed baking sheet. Bake for about 45 minutes until soft.

3 While the squash cooks, in a large pot over medium-high heat, heat the olive oil until it shimmers.

4 Add the onion. Cook for about 5 minutes, stirring occasionally, until soft.

5 Add the garlic and cook for 30 seconds, stirring constantly.

6 Stir in the crushed and chopped tomatoes, Italian seasoning, oregano, sea salt, and red pepper flakes. Bring to a simmer and reduce the heat to medium-low. Simmer for 10 minutes, stirring occasionally.

7 Once the squash is cooked, let it cool slightly before handling. Using a fork, scrape the flesh away from the rind into spaghetti-like noodles and place in a serving bowl.

8 Spoon the sauce over the squash and serve.

COOKING TIP: *To make the squash in a slow cooker, leave it whole and uncut. Prick the rind all over with a fork and place it in the cooker. Cook for 8 hours on low. No additional liquid is required, because the squash releases its own moisture. When done cooking, halve the squash and use a fork to scrape the flesh into strands.*

Per Serving Calories: 234; Protein: 7g; Total Carbohydrates: 35g; Sugars: 15g; Fiber: 8g; Total Fat: 9g; Saturated Fat: 1g; Cholesterol: 2mg; Sodium: 649mg

1 spaghetti squash, halved lengthwise and seeded

2 tablespoons extra-virgin olive oil

1 onion, chopped

6 garlic cloves, minced

2 (14-ounce) cans crushed tomatoes

1 (14-ounce) can chopped tomatoes, drained

1 tablespoon dried Italian seasoning

1 teaspoon dried oregano

½ teaspoon sea salt

¼ teaspoon red pepper flakes

Zucchini Noodles with Peas and Mint

Serves 6 ◆ **Prep time: 10 minutes** ◆ **Cook time: 15 minutes**

5 tablespoons
    extra-virgin olive
    oil, divided

1 shallot, minced

3 cups peas (fresh
    or frozen)

6 garlic cloves,
    minced

6 zucchini, spiralized
    into noodles

Juice of 1 lemon

Zest of 1 lemon

½ teaspoon sea salt

⅛ teaspoon freshly
    ground black
    pepper

¼ cup chopped fresh
    mint leaves

Zucchini noodles are becoming increasingly popular, and they're really easy to make. Many grocery stores now sell zucchini noodles in the produce section, or you can use a spiralizer to make them yourself. If you don't have a spiralizer, there's another way—see the tip for an alternative method for making the noodles without any special equipment.

1. In a large pot over medium-high heat, heat 3 tablespoons of olive oil until it shimmers.

2. Add the shallot. Cook for about 5 minutes, stirring occasionally, until soft.

3. Add the peas. Cook for 4 minutes, stirring occasionally.

4. Add the garlic and cook for 30 seconds, stirring constantly.

5. Add the zucchini, lemon juice and zest, sea salt, and pepper. Cook for about 4 minutes more, stirring, until the zucchini is al dente.

6. Toss with the remaining 2 tablespoons of olive oil and mint before serving.

COOKING TIP: *No spiralizer? No problem. Use a vegetable peeler to peel the zucchini (skin on) into long ribbon-like strips and use a sharp knife to cut the strips into noodles. Alternatively, leave the zucchini in ribbons for a slightly different shape and texture.*

Per Serving Calories: 225; Protein: 7g; Total Carbohydrates: 20g; Sugars: 8g; Fiber: 7g; Total Fat: 15g; Saturated Fat: 2g; Cholesterol: 0mg; Sodium: 261mg

Easy Zucchini Lasagna Wraps

Serves 6 • Prep time: 10 minutes • Cook time: 50 minutes

GLUTEN-FREE

VEGETARIAN

Using zucchini in place of lasagna noodles gives you the flavors of lasagna without all the carbs. To make the zucchini noodles, use a vegetable peeler and peel long strips from the zucchini. These freeze well, so they're great for making ahead.

1   Preheat the oven to 350°F.

2   In a large saucepan over medium-high heat, heat the olive oil until it shimmers.

3   Add the onion. Cook for about 5 minutes, stirring occasionally, until soft.

4   Add the garlic and cook for 30 seconds, stirring constantly.

5   Stir in the tomatoes, Italian seasoning, oregano, sea salt, and red pepper flakes. Simmer the sauce for 5 minutes, stirring occasionally.

6   In a 9-by-13-inch baking dish, roll each zucchini strip around 2 tablespoons of ricotta cheese. Place the rolls side by side in the baking dish. Top with the sauce and sprinkle with the mozzarella cheese. Bake for 35 to 40 minutes, uncovered, until the cheese browns and is bubbly.

MAKE IT A MEAL: *Serve this with Caprese Salad (page 112) for a satisfying and filling meal.*

Per Serving Calories: 286; Protein: 19g; Total Carbohydrates: 21g; Sugars: 11g; Fiber: 6g; Total Fat: 15g; Saturated Fat: 7g; Cholesterol: 39mg; Sodium: 642mg

2 tablespoons extra-virgin olive oil

1 onion, finely chopped

3 garlic cloves, minced

2 (14-ounce) cans crushed tomatoes

1 tablespoon dried Italian seasoning

1 teaspoon dried oregano

½ teaspoon sea salt

Pinch red pepper flakes

3 medium zucchini, peeled into long strips

2 cups low-fat ricotta cheese

½ cup grated part-skim mozzarella (about 4 ounces)

Spanakopita

Serves 8 ◦ **Prep time: 20 minutes** ◦ **Cook time: 1 hour**

6 tablespoons
   extra-virgin olive
   oil, divided

2 pounds fresh
   baby spinach

1 onion, chopped

12 ounces low-fat
   feta cheese

3 eggs, beaten

½ cup chopped
   fresh dill

½ teaspoon sea salt

1 pound phyllo
   pastry dough

Nonstick cooking
   spray

This crispy, savory Greek pastry feels like an indulgence, but it has enough good nutrition to balance the numbers. You can also cut the dough into different shapes, such as the popular triangle shape often associated with spanakopita. It keeps well—if you seal it very tightly and don't let air in, it will keep in the refrigerator for up to a week.

1   Preheat the oven to 375°F.

2   In a large skillet over medium-high heat, heat 1 tablespoon of olive oil until it shimmers.

3   Add the spinach and cook for about 2 minutes, stirring occasionally, until the spinach wilts. Transfer to a bowl and set aside.

4   Return the skillet to the heat and add another tablespoon of olive oil. Heat the oil until it shimmers.

5   Add the onion. Cook for 5 to 7 minutes, stirring occasionally, until soft. Add it to the bowl with the spinach, and let cool completely.

6   To the onion and spinach, add the feta, eggs, dill, and sea salt. Stir to combine.

7   Place the phyllo on a work surface and cover with a damp cloth. Keep the unused phyllo covered with the damp cloth as you work.

8   Spray a 12-inch-square baking pan with nonstick cooking spray.
     In the pan, place the phyllo sheets in layers, brushing each layer with
     the remaining 4 tablespoons of olive oil. Use half the phyllo to make
     the bottom layer.

9   Spread with the spinach mixture.

10   Layer the remaining phyllo on top, brushing olive oil between each
     layer. Using a sharp knife, score the top pastry layers to cut it into
     8 equal pieces. Don't cut through the bottom layer. Bake for 40 to
     45 minutes until golden brown.

COOKING TIP: *I place my pan directly on the oven floor for the last
15 to 20 minutes to make the spanakopita crispier. If you have an oven
with this capability, try it. Don't try this if you have a heating element on
the bottom of your oven—instead, set the oven to broil for 1 to 2 minutes
to crisp it a bit (but watch carefully—it can burn quickly).*

Per Serving Calories: 398; Protein: 18g; Total Carbohydrates: 39g; Sugars: 1g; Fiber: 4g; Total Fat: 21g;
Saturated Fat: 6g; Cholesterol: 77mg; Sodium: 1,027mg

Fish *and* Seafood

SHRIMP SCAMPI 152

SHRIMP MOJO DE AJO 153

PAN-SEARED SCALLOPS *with* SAUTÉED SPINACH 154

PAN-ROASTED SALMON *with* GREMOLATA 155

SALMON BURGERS 156

CRAB CAKES *with* SHAVED FENNEL SALAD 157

SWORDFISH KEBABS 158

CIOPPINO 159

HALIBUT EN PAPILLOTE *with* CAPERS,
ONIONS, OLIVES, *and* TOMATOES 160

POLLOCK *with* ROASTED TOMATOES 161

Left: Pollock with Roasted Tomatoes, p. 161

Shrimp Scampi

Serves 4 • Prep time: 10 minutes • Cook time: 15 minutes

Scampi is an irresistible combination of shrimp, garlic, and olive oil. Serve it over whole-wheat pasta, as suggested in this recipe, or enjoy it by itself alongside a salad and steamed veggies for a lighter, gluten-free option.

2 tablespoons extra-virgin olive oil

1 shallot, minced

1 pound medium shrimp, peeled, deveined, and tails removed

6 garlic cloves, minced

Juice of 1 lemon

Zest of 1 lemon

½ cup dry white wine

½ teaspoon sea salt

¼ teaspoon freshly ground black pepper

Pinch red pepper flakes

¼ cup chopped fresh Italian parsley leaves

6 ounces whole-wheat pasta, cooked according to package directions

1   In a large skillet over medium-high heat, heat the olive oil until it shimmers.

2   Add the shallot. Cook for about 5 minutes, stirring occasionally, until soft.

3   Toss in the shrimp. Cook for 3 to 4 minutes, stirring occasionally, until the shrimp is pink.

4   Add the garlic and cook for 30 seconds, stirring constantly.

5   Stir in the lemon juice and zest, wine, sea salt, pepper, and red pepper flakes. Bring to a simmer and reduce the heat to medium-low. Cook for about 2 minutes until the liquid reduces by half. Remove from the heat and stir in the parsley.

6   Toss with the hot pasta and serve.

VARIATION TIP: *This recipe also pairs nicely with spiralized zucchini or summer squash pasta, which is great if you're following a gluten-free diet. Use about 4 medium zucchini.*

Per Serving Calories: 394; Protein: 32g; Total Carbohydrates: 38g; Sugars: 2g; Fiber: 4g; Total Fat: 10g; Saturated Fat: 2g; Cholesterol: 239mg; Sodium: 524mg

Shrimp Mojo de Ajo

DAIRY-FREE
GLUTEN-FREE
MEAL IN ONE

Serves 4 ◆ Prep time: 10 minutes ◆ Cook time: 40 minutes

Intrigued? This recipe has a lot of garlic, but it cooks slowly and is sweet and mellow instead of sharp and strong. If you have a garlic press, it's a great way to process a lot of garlic very quickly. If not, pulse the garlic in a food processor to mince it quickly.

1   In a small saucepan over the lowest heat setting, bring the olive oil, garlic, and cayenne to a low simmer so bubbles just barely break the surface of the oil. Simmer for 30 minutes, stirring occasionally. Strain the garlic from the oil and set it aside.

2   Add the olive oil to a large skillet over medium-high heat and heat it until it shimmers.

3   Add the mushrooms. Cook for about 5 minutes, stirring once or twice, until browned.

4   Add the shrimp, lime juice, and sea salt. Cook for about 4 minutes, stirring occasionally, until the shrimp are pink.

5   Remove from the heat and stir in the cilantro and reserved garlic. Serve over the hot brown rice.

COOKING TIP: *To get the oil to simmer very lightly so you don't burn the garlic, use the smallest, least powerful burner and set it to its lowest setting. If the oil is still vigorously simmering or boiling, create a ring out of aluminum foil to lift the pan above the burner.*

Per Serving Calories: 354; Protein: 30g; Total Carbohydrates: 24g; Sugars: 1g; Fiber: 2g; Total Fat: 15g; Saturated Fat: 3g; Cholesterol: 239mg; Sodium: 518mg

¼ cup extra-virgin olive oil

10 garlic cloves, minced

⅛ teaspoon cayenne pepper, plus more as needed

8 ounces mushrooms, quartered

1 pound medium shrimp, peeled, deveined, and tails removed

Juice of 1 lime

½ teaspoon sea salt

¼ cup chopped fresh cilantro leaves

2 cups cooked brown rice

Pan-Seared Scallops with Sautéed Spinach

Serves 4 ◆ Prep time: 10 minutes ◆ Cook time: 15 minutes

1 pound sea scallops (see tip)

1 teaspoon sea salt, divided

½ teaspoon freshly ground black pepper, divided

2 tablespoons extra-virgin olive oil

6 cups fresh baby spinach

Juice of 1 orange

Pinch red pepper flakes

This decadent recipe calls for the larger sea scallops (not the pebble-size bay scallops). You'll serve these crispy-outside, tender-inside scallops on a bed of spinach, lightly scented with citrus.

1   Season the scallops on both sides with ½ teaspoon of sea salt and ¼ teaspoon of pepper.

2   In a large skillet over medium-high heat, heat the olive oil until it shimmers.

3   Add the scallops. Cook for 3 to 4 minutes per side without moving until browned. Remove the scallops from the skillet and set aside, tented with aluminum foil to keep warm.

4   Return the skillet to the heat and add the spinach, orange juice, red pepper flakes, remaining ½ teaspoon of salt, and remaining ¼ teaspoon of pepper. Cook for 4 to 5 minutes, stirring, until the spinach wilts.

5   Divide the spinach among 4 plates and top with the scallops. Serve immediately.

COOKING TIP: *Scallops have a tough tendon that runs along the outside. Rub alongside the scallop to feel for the tendon and remove it with a sharp knife before cooking.*

Per Serving Calories: 186; Protein: 21g; Total Carbohydrates: 8g; Sugars: 3g; Fiber: 2g; Total Fat: 8g; Saturated Fat: <1g; Cholesterol: 37mg; Sodium: 686mg

Pan-Roasted Salmon with Gremolata

DAIRY-FREE
GLUTEN-FREE
UNDER 30 MINUTES

Serves 6 • Prep time: 10 minutes • Cook time: 10 minutes

While the salmon cooks on the stove top and in the oven, you can prepare the gremolata, which is a quick and easy chopped herb condiment. Serve with a steamed veggie and starch of your choice, such as Sweet Potato Mash (page 127), for a full meal.

1   Preheat the oven to 350°F.

2   Season the salmon with ½ teaspoon of salt and the pepper.

3   In a large, ovenproof skillet over medium-high heat, heat the olive oil until it shimmers.

4   Add the salmon to the skillet, skin-side down. Cook for about 5 minutes, gently pressing on the salmon with a spatula, until the skin crisps. Transfer the pan to the oven and cook the salmon for 3 to 4 minutes more until it is opaque.

5   In a small bowl, stir together the parsley, garlic, lemon zest, and remaining ½ teaspoon of sea salt. Sprinkle the mixture over the salmon and serve.

COOKING TIP: *The best way to zest a lemon (or other citrus) is to use a handheld rasp-style grater (it looks like a nail file with holes). Carefully and lightly skim the lemon over the grater, removing only the yellow part and leaving the white pith, which can be quite bitter.*

Per Serving Calories: 214; Protein: 22g; Total Carbohydrates: <1g; Sugars: <1g; Fiber: <1g; Total Fat: 14g; Saturated Fat: 2g; Cholesterol: 50mg; Sodium: 522mg

1½ pounds skin-on salmon fillet, cut into 4 pieces

1 teaspoon sea salt, divided

¼ teaspoon freshly ground black pepper

3 tablespoons extra-virgin olive oil

1 bunch fresh Italian parsley leaves, finely chopped

1 garlic clove, minced

Zest of 1 lemon, finely grated (see tip)

Salmon Burgers

Serves 6 • Prep time: 10 minutes • Cook time: 10 minutes

16 ounces canned
  salmon, drained

6 scallions, white
  and green parts,
  finely chopped

¼ cup whole-wheat
  bread crumbs

2 eggs, beaten

2 tablespoons
  chopped
  fresh Italian
  parsley leaves

1 tablespoon dried
  Italian seasoning

Zest of 1 lemon

2 tablespoons extra-
  virgin olive oil

¼ cup unsweetened
  nonfat plain
  Greek yogurt

1 tablespoon chopped
  fresh dill

1 tablespoon
  capers, rinsed
  and chopped

¼ teaspoon sea salt

6 whole-wheat
  hamburger buns

Make burger night more interesting—and healthy—with these tasty salmon burgers. I've included an easy homemade sauce for them that adds a boatload of flavor. Finish with your favorite burger fixings, such as lettuce, sliced onions, or sliced tomatoes.

1   In a medium bowl, mix together the salmon, scallions, bread crumbs, eggs, parsley, Italian seasoning, and lemon zest. Form the mixture into 6 patties about ½-inch thick.

2   In a large nonstick skillet over medium-high heat, heat the olive oil until it shimmers.

3   Add the salmon patties. Cook for about 4 minutes per side until browned.

4   While the salmon cooks, in a small bowl, whisk the yogurt, dill, capers, and sea salt. Spread the sauce on the buns. Top with the patties and serve.

MAKE IT A MEAL: *To really treat yourself, serve these burgers with a salad and a side of sweet potato fries. To make the fries, cut 2 sweet potatoes into ½-inch-thick sticks. Toss with 2 tablespoons extra-virgin olive oil and ½ teaspoon sea salt. Spread in a single layer on a rimmed baking sheet. Bake at 450°F for about 20 minutes, turning occasionally, until the fries are crisp on the outside and tender on the inside.*

Per Serving Calories: 319; Protein: 28g; Total Carbohydrates: 24g; Sugars: 6g; Fiber: 3g; Total Fat: 13g; Saturated Fat: 2g; Cholesterol: 95mg; Sodium: 344mg

Crab Cakes with Shaved Fennel Salad

GLUTEN-FREE

MEAL IN ONE

UNDER 30 MINUTES

Serves 6 ◆ Prep time: 20 minutes ◆ Cook time: 10 minutes

These crab cakes are simple and flavorful. Instead of using bread crumbs as a binder, they use shrimp mousse, which adds flavor and holds the lump crabmeat together easily. Enjoy this treat from the sea over a salad, on a whole-wheat hamburger bun, or by itself!

1   In a blender or food processor, blend the shrimp, heavy cream, ½ teaspoon of sea salt, and ⅛ teaspoon of pepper until smooth.

2   In a large bowl, stir together the crabmeat and scallions.

3   Fold in the shrimp mousse until well mixed. Form the mixture into 8 patties. Refrigerate for 10 minutes.

4   In a large, nonstick skillet over medium-high heat, heat 2 tablespoons of olive oil until it shimmers.

5   Add the crab cakes. Cook for about 4 minutes per side until browned on both sides.

6   In a large bowl, combine the fennel and fennel fronds.

7   In a small bowl, whisk the remaining 2 tablespoons of olive oil with the lemon juice, mustard, garlic, and remaining ½ teaspoon of sea salt, and ⅛ teaspoon of pepper. Toss the dressing with the fennel and serve with the crab cakes.

COOKING TIP: *If you have a mandoline, save some time by setting it to ⅛ inch and shaving the fennel. You can also use the shaving part of a box grater, or use a slicer in a food processor.*

INGREDIENT TIP: *If you're really watching your fat intake and want to cut the saturated fat from this dish, replace the heavy (whipping) cream with an equal amount of skim milk. Be aware that the crab cakes may not hold together as well as when made with the cream.*

Per Serving Calories: 379; Protein: 35g; Total Carbohydrates: 10g; Sugars: <1g; Fiber: 3g; Total Fat: 20g; Saturated Fat: 4g; Cholesterol: 250mg; Sodium: 1,434mg

¾ cup cooked baby shrimp

3 tablespoons heavy (whipping) cream

1 teaspoon sea salt, divided

¼ teaspoon freshly ground black pepper, divided

1½ pounds lump crabmeat

6 scallions, white and green parts, thinly sliced

¼ cup extra-virgin olive oil, divided

3 fennel bulbs, cored and very thinly sliced

2 tablespoons chopped fennel fronds

¼ cup freshly squeezed lemon juice

½ teaspoon Dijon mustard

1 garlic clove, minced

Swordfish Kebabs

Serves 6 ◆ Prep time: 20 minutes ◆ Cook time: 10 minutes

3 tablespoons extra-
virgin olive oil,
plus more for
the grill

Juice of 2 oranges

1 tablespoon
Dijon mustard

2 teaspoons dried
tarragon

½ teaspoon sea salt

⅛ teaspoon freshly
ground black
pepper

2 pounds swordfish,
cut into 1½-inch
pieces

2 red bell peppers,
cut into pieces

Swordfish is a hearty, flavorful, filling fish. Here, it combines with
an herb marinade and veggies for a tasty main course. Fish marinates
quickly—you'll need only about 10 minutes for it to soak up the flavors
of the marinade.

1   In a medium bowl, whisk the olive oil, orange juice, mustard,
tarragon, sea salt, and pepper.

2   Add the swordfish and toss to coat. Let sit for 10 minutes.

3   Heat a grill or grill pan to medium-high heat and brush it with oil.

4   Thread the swordfish and red bell peppers onto 6 wooden skewers
(see tip). Cook for 6 to 8 minutes, turning, until the fish is opaque.

MAKE IT A MEAL: *Serve these kebabs with Rice and Spinach (page 125)
to make a full meal.*

PREPARATION TIP: *Soak your wooden skewers in water before threading
the food on them to prevent burning on the grill.*

Per Serving Calories: 326; Protein: 33g; Total Carbohydrates: 11g; Sugars: 8g; Fiber: 2g; Total Fat: 18g;
Saturated Fat: 1g; Cholesterol: 0mg; Sodium: 187mg

Cioppino

DAIRY-FREE
GLUTEN-FREE
MEAL IN ONE
UNDER 30 MINUTES

Serves 8 • **Prep time: 10 minutes** • **Cook time: 15 minutes**

Cioppino is a hearty and oh-so-versatile seafood stew. Customize this dish using the types of seafood you enjoy—I love shellfish. Just swap out the cod and salmon for an equal proportion of clams, mussels, sea scallops, and/or lobster. Serve with crusty whole-wheat bread and a side salad for an unforgettable meal.

1 In a large pot over medium-high heat, heat the olive oil until it shimmers.

2 Add the onion and fennel. Cook for about 5 minutes, stirring occasionally, until the vegetables are soft.

3 Add the garlic and cook for 30 seconds, stirring constantly.

4 Stir in the wine and cook for 1 minute, stirring constantly.

5 Add the tomato sauce, broth, shrimp, cod, salmon, Italian seasoning, sea salt, red pepper flakes, and pepper. Bring to a simmer and reduce the heat to medium-low. Cook for about 5 minutes more, stirring occasionally, until the fish and shrimp are opaque.

6 Remove from heat and stir in the basil before serving.

INGREDIENT TIP: *The salmon and cod may have small pin bones. Using needlenose pliers, carefully remove any bones you see and discard them.*

Per Serving Calories: 326; Protein: 40g; Total Carbohydrates: 18g; Sugars: 11g; Fiber: 4g; Total Fat: 10g; Saturated Fat: 1g; Cholesterol: 178mg; Sodium: 1,529mg

2 tablespoons extra-virgin olive oil

1 onion, chopped

1 fennel bulb, chopped

6 garlic cloves, minced

½ cup dry white wine

2 (32-ounce) cans tomato sauce

2 cups unsalted chicken broth

1 pound shrimp, peeled, deveined, and tails removed

1 pound cod, cut into bite-size pieces

1 pound salmon, skin removed, cut into bite-size pieces

2 tablespoons Italian seasoning

½ teaspoon sea salt

⅛ teaspoon red pepper flakes

⅛ teaspoon freshly ground black pepper

¼ cup chopped fresh basil leaves

Halibut en Papillote with Capers, Onions, Olives, and Tomatoes

DAIRY-FREE

GLUTEN-FREE

MEAL IN ONE

UNDER 30 MINUTES

Serves 4 ◆ Prep time: 10 minutes ◆ Cook time: 8 minutes

4 (6-ounce) halibut
   fillets

2 tablespoons extra-
   virgin olive oil

½ teaspoon sea salt

¼ teaspoon freshly
   ground black
   pepper

⅛ teaspoon crushed
   red pepper flakes

2 garlic cloves, thinly
   sliced

1 cup grape
   tomatoes, halved

¼ cup chopped onion

2 tablespoons
   capers, drained

8 Kalamata olives,
   pitted and
   quartered

2 tablespoons plus
   2 teaspoons dry
   white wine

8 fresh thyme sprigs

After savoring this dish at a Mediterranean restaurant in New York, I knew I had to figure out how to replicate it at home using fresh ingredients I love. Halibut is a very meaty fish—it feels like you're eating more than you are, which comes in handy when you're dieting!

1 Cut 4 (15-inch) squares of parchment paper or aluminum foil. Set aside.

2 Preheat the oven to 450°F.

3 Brush the halibut with the olive oil and sprinkle with the sea salt, pepper, and red pepper flakes. Place each fillet on a parchment square.

4 Layer the fillets with the garlic, tomatoes, onion, capers, and olives. Fold into packets, leaving the tops open.

5 Add 2 teaspoons white wine to each packet along with a thyme sprig. Seal the packets and place them on a rimmed baking sheet. Bake for about 8 minutes until the fish is opaque. Serve immediately.

SUBSTITUTION TIP: *If halibut is not available, use any other white-fleshed fish, such as cod.*

Per Serving Calories: 181; Protein: 26g; Total Carbohydrates: 3g; Sugars: 1g; Fiber: <1; Total Fat: 6g; Saturated Fat: 1g; Cholesterol: 62mg; Sodium: 383mg

Pollock with Roasted Tomatoes

Serves 6 • Prep time: 5 minutes • Cook time: 40 minutes

Toasted whole-wheat bread crumbs give a toasty crunch to
mild pollock, which sits on a bed of roasted tomatoes. You can
prepare the pollock and bread crumbs on the stove top while the
tomatoes roast.

1   Preheat the oven to 450°F.

2   In a large bowl, toss the tomatoes, shallots, and garlic with 1 tablespoon
    of olive oil, ½ teaspoon of sea salt, and ¼ teaspoon of pepper. Transfer
    to a rimmed baking sheet and arrange in a single layer. Bake for about
    40 minutes until the tomatoes are soft and browned.

3   While the tomatoes cook, in a large nonstick skillet over medium-high
    heat, heat 1 tablespoon plus 1 teaspoon of olive oil until it bubbles.

4   Add the bread crumbs and cook for about 5 minutes, stirring, until they
    are browned and crunchy. Remove from the pan and set aside, scraping
    the pan clean.

5   Return the skillet to medium-high heat and add the remaining table-
    spoon of olive oil.

6   Season the fish with the remaining ½ teaspoon of sea salt and
    ¼ teaspoon of pepper. Place the fish in the skillet. Cook for about
    5 minutes per side until opaque.

7   To assemble, spoon the tomatoes onto four plates. Top with the pollock
    and sprinkle with the bread crumbs. Garnish with parsley and serve.

VARIATION TIP: *If you can't find pollock, use any white-fleshed fish,
such as cod or halibut.*

INGREDIENT TIP: *If you'd like to cut the saturated fat from this recipe,
use olive oil instead of butter.*

Per Serving Calories: 286; Protein: 30g; Total Carbohydrates: 22g; Sugars: 7g; Fiber: 3g; Total Fat: 9g;
Saturated Fat: 2g; Cholesterol: 64mg; Sodium: 419mg

12 plum tomatoes,
    halved

2 shallots, very thinly
    cut into rings

3 garlic cloves,
    minced

3 tablespoons plus
    1 teaspoon
    extra-virgin olive
    oil, divided

1 teaspoon sea
    salt, divided

½ teaspoon freshly
    ground black
    pepper, divided

1 teaspoon butter
    (or extra-virgin
    olive oil)

¾ cup whole-wheat
    bread crumbs

6 (4-ounce) pollock
    fillets

¼ cup chopped fresh
    Italian parsley
    leaves

12

Poultry *and* Meat

TURKEY BURGERS *with* **MANGO SALSA**   164

HERB-ROASTED TURKEY BREAST   165

CHICKEN SAUSAGE *and* **PEPPERS**   166

CHICKEN PICCATA   167

ONE-PAN TUSCAN CHICKEN   168

CHICKEN KAPAMA   169

SPINACH *and* **FETA-STUFFED CHICKEN BREASTS**   170

ROSEMARY BAKED CHICKEN DRUMSTICKS   171

CHICKEN *with* **POTATOES, FIGS,** *and* **CARROTS**   172

CHICKEN GYROS *with* **TZATZIKI**   173

MOUSSAKA   174

DIJON *and* **HERB PORK TENDERLOIN**   175

STEAK *with* **RED WINE-MUSHROOM SAUCE**   176

GREEK MEATBALLS (KEFTEDES)   178

LAMB *with* **STRING BEANS (ARNI ME FASOLAKIA)**   179

Left: Chicken with Potatoes, Figs, and Carrots, p. 172

Turkey Burgers with Mango Salsa

DAIRY-FREE

GLUTEN-FREE

UNDER 30 MINUTES

1½ pounds ground turkey breast

1 teaspoon sea salt, divided

¼ teaspoon freshly ground black pepper

2 tablespoons extra-virgin olive oil

2 mangos, peeled, pitted, and cubed

½ red onion, finely chopped

Juice of 1 lime

1 garlic clove, minced

½ jalapeño pepper, seeded and finely minced

2 tablespoons chopped fresh cilantro leaves

Serves 6 ◆ Prep time: 15 minutes ◆ Cook time: 10 minutes

Serve these burgers on gluten-free buns, or wrap them in a lettuce leaf and top with the flavorful salsa. Add a side salad, and you've got a delicious and satisfying meal. The patties will keep in the freezer for up to six months or in the refrigerator for about three days. The salsa will keep for a day or two in the refrigerator.

1. Form the turkey breast into 4 patties and season with ½ teaspoon of sea salt and the pepper.

2. In a large nonstick skillet over medium-high heat, heat the olive oil until it shimmers.

3. Add the turkey patties and cook for about 5 minutes per side until browned.

4. While the patties cook, mix together the mango, red onion, lime juice, garlic, jalapeño, cilantro, and remaining ½ teaspoon of sea salt in a small bowl. Spoon the salsa over the turkey patties and serve.

VARIATION TIP: *Serve this salsa over grilled halibut. Heat the grill to medium-high heat and brush it with olive oil. Grill 4 (4- to 6-ounce) halibut fillets for about 6 minutes per side. Top with the salsa.*

Per Serving Calories: 384; Protein: 34g; Total Carbohydrates: 27g; Sugars: 24g; Fiber: 3g; Total Fat: 16g; Saturated Fat: 3g; Cholesterol: 84mg; Sodium: 543mg

Herb-Roasted Turkey Breast

DAIRY-FREE

GLUTEN-FREE

Serves 6 • Prep time: 15 minutes • Cook time: 1½ hours (plus 20 minutes to rest)

Fresh herbs add tons of fragrance and flavor to the turkey breast. If you don't want to spend the time chopping the herbs, pulse them in a blender or food processor until well chopped and blended, 10 to 20 (1-second) pulses. Freeze leftovers for up to six months or refrigerate them for up to five days and use them in sandwiches, on salads, or for other meals.

1 Preheat the oven to 325°F.

2 In a small bowl, whisk the olive oil, garlic, lemon zest, thyme, rosemary, parsley, mustard, sea salt, and pepper. Spread the herb mixture evenly over the surface of the turkey breast, and loosen the skin and rub underneath as well. Place the turkey breast in a roasting pan on a rack, skin-side up.

3 Pour the wine in the pan. Roast for 1 to 1½ hours until the turkey reaches an internal temperature of 165°F. Remove from the oven and let rest for 20 minutes, tented with aluminum foil to keep it warm, before carving.

MAKE IT A MEAL: *Serve alongside Sweet Potato Mash (page 127) and Easy Brussels Sprouts Hash (page 182) for a complete meal.*

Per Serving Calories: 392; Protein: 84g; Total Carbohydrates: 2g; Sugars: <1g; Fiber: <1g; Total Fat: 6g; Saturated Fat: <1g; Cholesterol: 210mg; Sodium: 479mg

2 tablespoons extra-virgin olive oil

4 garlic cloves, minced

Zest of 1 lemon

1 tablespoon chopped fresh thyme leaves

1 tablespoon chopped fresh rosemary leaves

2 tablespoons chopped fresh Italian parsley leaves

1 teaspoon ground mustard

1 teaspoon sea salt

¼ teaspoon freshly ground black pepper

1 (6-pound) bone-in, skin-on turkey breast

1 cup dry white wine

Chicken Sausage and Peppers

Serves 6 ◆ Prep time: 10 minutes ◆ Cook time: 20 minutes

2 tablespoons extra-
virgin olive oil

6 Italian chicken
sausage links

1 onion, thinly sliced

1 red bell pepper,
seeded and
thinly sliced

1 green bell pepper,
seeded and
thinly sliced

3 garlic cloves,
minced

½ cup dry white wine

½ teaspoon sea salt

¼ teaspoon freshly
ground black
pepper

Pinch red pepper
flakes

This traditional Italian-American dish is flavorful and satisfying.
Pop these sausages and peppers on buns as sandwiches, or serve
them alongside your favorite salad for a complete meal.

1   In a large skillet over medium-high heat, heat the olive oil until
it shimmers.

2   Add the sausages and cook for 5 to 7 minutes, turning occasionally,
until browned, and they reach an internal temperature of 165°F.
With tongs, remove the sausage from the pan and set aside on a platter,
tented with aluminum foil to keep warm.

3   Return the skillet to the heat and add the onion, red bell pepper,
and green bell pepper. Cook for 5 to 7 minutes, stirring occasionally,
until the vegetables begin to brown.

4   Add the garlic and cook for 30 seconds, stirring constantly.

5   Stir in the wine, sea salt, pepper, and red pepper flakes. Use the side
of a spoon to scrape and fold in any browned bits from the bottom of the
pan. Simmer for about 4 minutes more, stirring, until the liquid reduces
by half. Spoon the peppers over the sausages and serve.

SUBSTITUTION TIP: *For a different flavor profile, add 1 fennel bulb, thinly
shaved, in place of the green bell peppers. Cook as directed in the recipe.*

Per Serving Calories: 173; Protein: 22g; Total Carbohydrates: 6g; Sugars: 2g; Fiber: <1g; Total Fat: 5g;
Saturated Fat: 1g; Cholesterol: 85mg; Sodium: 1,199mg

Chicken Piccata

DAIRY-FREE

UNDER 30 MINUTES

Serves 6 ◆ **Prep time: 10 minutes** ◆ **Cook time: 15 minutes**

This Italian favorite is made with chicken breasts and a light, flavorful pan sauce. Chicken piccata is an easy and delicious meal for week-nights because it's ready in a snap, especially with the chicken pounded nice and thin.

1 In a shallow dish, whisk the flour, sea salt, and pepper. Dredge the chicken in the flour and tap off any excess.

2 In a large skillet over medium-high heat, heat the olive oil until it shimmers.

3 Add the chicken and cook for about 4 minutes per side until browned. Remove the chicken from the pan and set aside, tented with aluminum foil to keep warm.

4 Return the skillet to the heat and add the broth, wine, lemon juice, and lemon zest, and capers. Use the side of a spoon to scrape and fold in any browned bits from the bottom of the pan. Simmer for 3 to 4 minutes, stirring, until the liquid thickens. Remove the skillet from the heat and return the chicken to the pan. Turn to coat. Stir in the parsley and serve.

COOKING TIP: *To pound the chicken to an even thickness: Place the chicken between two pieces of plastic wrap or parchment paper and use a flat kitchen mallet or a smooth-bottomed heavy saucepan to pound until they reach the desired thickness. Use caution to avoid puncturing the plastic or paper.*

Per Serving Calories: 153; Protein: 8g; Total Carbohydrates: 9g; Sugars: <1g; Fiber: <1g; Total Fat: 9g; Saturated Fat: 1g; Cholesterol: 19mg; Sodium: 352mg

½ cup whole-wheat flour

½ teaspoon sea salt

⅛ teaspoon freshly ground black pepper

1½ pounds boneless, skinless chicken breasts, cut into 6 pieces and pounded ½-inch thick (see tip)

3 tablespoons extra-virgin olive oil

1 cup unsalted chicken broth

½ cup dry white wine

Juice of 1 lemon

Zest of 1 lemon

¼ cup capers, drained and rinsed

¼ cup chopped fresh parsley leaves

One-Pan Tuscan Chicken

Serves 6 • Prep time: 10 minutes • Cook time: 25 minutes

¼ cup extra-virgin olive oil, divided

1 pound boneless, skinless chicken breasts, cut into ¾-inch pieces

1 onion, chopped

1 red bell pepper, chopped

3 garlic cloves, minced

½ cup dry white wine

1 (14-ounce) can crushed tomatoes, undrained

1 (14-ounce) can chopped tomatoes, drained

1 (14-ounce) can white beans, drained

1 tablespoon dried Italian seasoning

½ teaspoon sea salt

⅛ teaspoon freshly ground black pepper

⅛ teaspoon red pepper flakes

¼ cup chopped fresh basil leaves

This fragrant chicken skillet will transport you to Italy's Tuscany region as its aromas fill the air. It also cooks quickly and is a meal all by itself. This keeps well—it can easily be frozen and reheated, and you can refrigerate it for about three days. Freeze it in single servings for meals on the go.

1   In a large skillet over medium-high heat, heat 2 tablespoons of olive oil until it shimmers.

2   Add the chicken and cook for about 6 minutes, stirring, until browned. Remove the chicken from the skillet and set aside on a platter, tented with aluminum foil to keep warm.

3   Return the skillet to the heat and heat the remaining 2 tablespoons of olive oil until it shimmers.

4   Add the onion and red bell pepper. Cook for about 5 minutes, stirring occasionally, until the vegetables are soft.

5   Add the garlic and cook for 30 seconds, stirring constantly.

6   Stir in the wine, and use the side of the spoon to scrape and fold in any browned bits from the bottom of the pan. Cook for 1 minute, stirring.

7   Add the crushed and chopped tomatoes, white beans, Italian seasoning, sea salt, pepper, and red pepper flakes. Bring to a simmer and reduce the heat to medium. Cook for 5 minutes, stirring occasionally.

8   Return the chicken and any juices that have collected to the skillet. Cook for 1 to 2 minutes until the chicken heats through. Remove from the heat and stir in the basil before serving.

VARIATION TIP: *Add ½ cup chopped black or green olives and 1 cup thawed frozen spinach when you return the chicken to the pan. Note that the fat content will increase.*

Per Serving Calories: 271; Protein: 14g; Total Carbohydrates: 29g; Sugars: 8g; Fiber: 8g; Total Fat: 0g; Saturated Fat: 1g; Cholesterol: 14mg; Sodium: 306mg

Chicken Kapama

DAIRY-FREE
GLUTEN-FREE
MEAL IN ONE

Serves 4 ⋄ Prep time: 10 minutes ⋄ Cook time: 2 hours

Chicken kapama is a baked chicken dish with a spiced tomato sauce containing unexpected flavors such as cinnamon and allspice. Make the sauce before the chicken (you can make it up to three days ahead and refrigerate it), and pour it over the chicken just before baking.

1   In a large pot over medium-high heat, combine the tomatoes, wine, tomato paste, olive oil, red pepper flakes, allspice, oregano, cloves, cinnamon stick, sea salt, and pepper. Bring to a simmer, stirring occasionally. Reduce the heat to medium-low and simmer for 30 minutes, stirring occasionally. Remove and discard the whole cloves and cinnamon stick from the sauce and let the sauce cool.

2   Preheat the oven to 350°F.

3   Place the chicken in a 9-by-13-inch baking dish. Pour the sauce over the chicken and cover the pan with aluminum foil. Bake for 40 to 45 minutes, or until the chicken reaches an internal temperature of 165°F.

MAKE IT A MEAL: *Serve this dish spooned over ¾ cup (per serving) cooked whole-wheat pasta.*

Per Serving Calories: 220; Protein: 8g; Total Carbohydrates: 11g; Sugars: 7g; Fiber: 3g; Total Fat: 14g; Saturated Fat: 3g; Cholesterol: 19mg; Sodium: 273mg

1 (32-ounce) can chopped tomatoes, drained

¼ cup dry white wine

2 tablespoons tomato paste

3 tablespoons extra-virgin olive oil

¼ teaspoon red pepper flakes

1 teaspoon ground allspice

½ teaspoon dried oregano

2 whole cloves

1 cinnamon stick

½ teaspoon sea salt

⅛ teaspoon freshly ground black pepper

4 boneless, skinless chicken breast halves

Spinach and Feta–Stuffed Chicken Breasts

2 tablespoons extra-virgin olive oil

1 pound fresh baby spinach

3 garlic cloves, minced

Zest of 1 lemon

½ teaspoon sea salt

⅛ teaspoon freshly ground black pepper

½ cup crumbled feta cheese

4 boneless, skinless chicken breast halves, pounded to ½-inch thickness

Serves 4 ◆ Prep time: 10 minutes ◆ Cook time: 45 minutes

Stuffing a chicken breast is a fantastic way to add flavor and texture. This baked version uses spinach and feta cheese, although you can add your own flavor embellishments, such as herbs and spices, to the filling.

1 Preheat the oven to 350°F.

2 In a large skillet over medium-high heat, heat the olive oil until it shimmers.

3 Add the spinach. Cook for 3 to 4 minutes, stirring, until wilted.

4 Add the garlic, lemon zest, sea salt, and pepper. Cook for 30 seconds, stirring constantly. Cool slightly and mix in the cheese.

5 Spread the spinach and cheese mixture in an even layer over the chicken pieces and roll the breast around the filling. Hold closed with tooth-picks or butcher's twine. Place the breasts in a 9-by-13-inch baking dish and bake for 30 to 40 minutes, or until the chicken reaches an internal temperature of 165°F. Remove from the oven and let rest for 5 minutes before slicing and serving.

COOKING TIP: *If you use toothpicks to hold the chicken rolls closed, soak them in water for about 5 minutes first to prevent burning.*

Per Serving Calories: 263; Protein: 17g; Total Carbohydrates: 7g; Sugars: 3g; Fiber: 3g; Total Fat: 20g; Saturated Fat: 9g; Cholesterol: 63mg; Sodium: 901mg

Rosemary Baked Chicken Drumsticks

DAIRY-FREE
GLUTEN-FREE

Serves 6 • **Prep time: 5 minutes** • **Cook time: 1 hour**

In other cultures, many people prefer dark meat over chicken breasts—it's more juicy and flavorful. Although baking time is an hour here, these drumsticks are otherwise fast and easy. You can refrigerate leftovers for up to three days and they make excellent next-day lunches.

1   Preheat the oven to 350°F.

2   In a small bowl, combine the rosemary, garlic powder, sea salt, pepper, and lemon zest.

3   Place the drumsticks in a 9-by-13-inch baking dish and sprinkle with the rosemary mixture. Bake for about 1 hour, or until the chicken reaches an internal temperature of 165°F.

MAKE IT A MEAL: *Serve with Mashed Cauliflower (page 185) and Citrus Sautéed Spinach (page 184) for a complete meal.*

Per Serving Calories: 163; Protein: 26g; Total Carbohydrates: 2g; Sugars: <1g; Fiber: <1g; Total Fat: 6g; Saturated Fat: 2g; Cholesterol: 81mg; Sodium: 309mg

2 tablespoons chopped fresh rosemary leaves

1 teaspoon garlic powder

½ teaspoon sea salt

⅛ teaspoon freshly ground black pepper

Zest of 1 lemon

12 chicken drumsticks

DAIRY-FREE

GLUTEN-FREE

MEAL IN ONE

2 cups fingerling
   potatoes, halved

4 fresh figs,
   quartered

2 carrots, julienned

2 tablespoons extra-
   virgin olive oil

1 teaspoon sea salt,
   divided

¼ teaspoon freshly
   ground black
   pepper

4 chicken leg-thigh
   quarters

2 tablespoons
   chopped fresh
   parsley leaves

Chicken with Potatoes, Figs, and Carrots

Serves 4 • Prep time: 5 minutes • Cook time: 45 minutes

Figs are high in fiber and key minerals, such as copper, manganese, and potassium. This dish bakes in one pan, and there's minimal cleanup. The result is a delicious meal with lots of flavor.

1   Preheat the oven to 425°F.

2   In a small bowl, toss the potatoes, figs, and carrots with the olive oil, ½ teaspoon of sea salt, and the pepper. Spread in a 9-by-13-inch baking dish.

3   Season the chicken with the remaining ½ teaspoon of sea salt. Place it on top of the vegetables. Bake for 35 to 45 minutes, or until the vegetables are soft and the chicken reaches an internal temperature of 165°F.

4   Sprinkle with the parsley and serve.

VARIATION TIP: *Use 8 chicken drumsticks if you can't find leg-thigh quarters.*

Per Serving Calories: 429; Protein: 52g; Total Carbohydrates: 27g; Sugars: 12g; Fiber: 4g; Total Fat: 12g; Saturated Fat: 3g; Cholesterol: 131mg; Sodium: 603mg

Chicken Gyros with Tzatziki

GLUTEN

Serves 6 ◦ Prep time: 10 minutes ◦ Cook time: 1 hour (plus 20 minutes to rest)

You can find these snacks on every corner in Greece. This classic street food is to Greece what the hot dog is to America. It's fun to watch the vendor carve the chicken and prepare the gyro right in front of you. Oh, and they're good—and good for you!

1 Preheat the oven to 350°F.

2 In a stand mixer or food processor, combine the chicken, onion, rosemary, marjoram, garlic, sea salt, and pepper. Blend for about 2 minutes until the mixture forms a paste. Alternatively, mix these ingredients in a bowl until well combined (see preparation tip).

3 Press the mixture into a loaf pan. Bake for about 1 hour until it reaches an internal temperature of 165°F. Remove from the oven and let rest for 20 minutes before slicing.

4 Slice the gyro and spoon the tzatziki sauce over the top.

PREPARATION TIP: *This recipe works best if you have a food processor or stand mixer, because it allows you to process the meat into a thick paste, which is what you want for the traditional gyro texture. However, if you don't have these appliances, mix together all the ingredients in a bowl until well combined. The texture will be more like a meatloaf, but the flavors will be the same.*

INGREDIENT TIP: *To wring excess water from an onion, grate it, then wrap it in a clean kitchen towel. Wring the towel over the sink until no more water drips from it.*

Per Serving Calories: 289; Protein: 50g; Total Carbohydrates: 20g; Sugars: 10g; Fiber: 1g; Total Fat: 1g; Saturated Fat: <1g; Cholesterol: 67mg; Sodium: 494mg

1 pound
    chicke   east

1 onion, grated
    with excess
    water wrung out
    (see tip)

2 tablespoons dried
    rosemary

1 tablespoon dried
    marjoram

6 garlic cloves,
    minced

½ teaspoon sea salt

¼ teaspoon freshly
    ground black
    pepper

Tzatziki Sauce
    (see page 106)

Moussaka

Serves 8 • Prep time: 10 minutes • Cook time: 45 minutes

This is my favorite traditional Greek meal. Every time I want to splurge at a Greek bazaar or restaurant, I choose this indulgence. This recipe has been transformed into a healthier version so it can be enjoyed more frequently without guilt.

1   Preheat the oven to 400°F.

2   In a large skillet over medium-high heat, heat 3 tablespoons of olive oil until it shimmers.

3   Add the eggplant slices and brown for 3 to 4 minutes per side. Transfer to paper towels to drain.

4   Return the skillet to the heat and add the remaining 2 tablespoons of olive oil. Add the onion and green bell pepper. Cook for about 5 minutes, stirring, until the vegetables are soft. Remove from the pan and set aside.

5   Return the skillet to the heat and add the turkey. Cook for about 5 minutes, crumbling with a spoon, until browned.

6   Add the garlic and cook for 30 seconds, stirring constantly.

7   Stir in the tomato paste, tomatoes, Italian seasoning, Worcestershire sauce, oregano, and cinnamon. Return the onion and bell pepper to the pan. Cook for 5 minutes, stirring.

8   In a small bowl, whisk the yogurt, egg, pepper, nutmeg, and cheese.

9   In a 9-by-13-inch baking dish, spread half the meat mixture. Layer with half the eggplant. Add the remaining meat mixture and the remaining eggplant. Spread with the yogurt mixture. Bake for about 20 minutes until golden brown.

10 Garnish with the parsley and serve.

VARIATION TIP: *Use extra-lean ground beef in place of the ground turkey.*

Per Serving Calories: 338; Protein: 28g; Total Carbohydrates: 16g; Sugars: 10g; Fiber: 5g; Total Fat: 20g; Saturated Fat: 4g; Cholesterol: 110mg; Sodium: 194mg

Ingredients

5 tablespoons extra-virgin olive oil, divided

1 eggplant, sliced (unpeeled)

1 onion, chopped

1 green bell pepper, seeded and chopped

1 pound ground turkey

3 garlic cloves, minced

2 tablespoons tomato paste

1 (14-ounce) can chopped tomatoes, drained

1 tablespoon Italian seasoning

2 teaspoons Worcestershire sauce

1 teaspoon dried oregano

½ teaspoon ground cinnamon

1 cup unsweetened nonfat plain Greek yogurt

1 egg, beaten

¼ teaspoon freshly ground black pepper

¼ teaspoon ground nutmeg

¼ cup grated Parmesan cheese

2 tablespoons chopped fresh parsley leaves

Dijon and Herb Pork Tenderloin

DAIRY-FREE
GLUTEN-FREE

Serves 6 ◦ **Prep time: 10 minutes** ◦
Cook time: 20 minutes (plus 10 minutes to rest)

This simple pork tenderloin requires very little active time, but the end result tastes like you spent hours in the kitchen. If you like, rub the herb crust on the tenderloin in the morning and allow it to rest in the refrigerator in a large resealable bag all day before you cook it.

1   Preheat the oven to 400°F.

2   In a blender or food processor, combine the parsley, rosemary, thyme, mustard, olive oil, garlic, sea salt, and pepper. Process for about 30 seconds until smooth. Spread the mixture evenly over the pork and place it on a rimmed baking sheet.

3   Bake for about 20 minutes, or until the meat reaches an internal temperature of 140°F. Remove from the oven and let rest for 10 minutes before slicing and serving.

COOKING TIP: *A digital instant-read thermometer is a great tool for measuring internal temperature. Take the temperature at the thickest part of the meat by inserting the probe just to the center.*

Per Serving Calories: 393; Protein: 74g; Total Carbohydrates: 5g; Sugars: <1g; Fiber: 3g; Total Fat: 12g; Saturated Fat: 4g; Cholesterol: 167mg; Sodium: 617mg

½ cup fresh Italian parsley leaves, chopped

3 tablespoons fresh rosemary leaves, chopped

3 tablespoons fresh thyme leaves, chopped

3 tablespoons Dijon mustard

1 tablespoon extra-virgin olive oil

4 garlic cloves, minced

½ teaspoon sea salt

¼ teaspoon freshly ground black pepper

1 (1½-pound) pork tenderloin

Steak with Red Wine–Mushroom Sauce

FOR THE MARINADE AND STEAK

1 cup dry red wine

3 garlic cloves, minced

2 tablespoons extra-virgin olive oil

1 tablespoon low-sodium soy sauce

1 tablespoon dried thyme

1 teaspoon Dijon mustard

2 tablespoons extra-virgin olive oil

1 to 1½ pounds skirt steak, flat iron steak, or tri-tip steak

FOR THE MUSHROOM SAUCE

2 tablespoons extra-virgin olive oil

1 pound cremini mushrooms, quartered

½ teaspoon sea salt

1 teaspoon dried thyme

⅛ teaspoon freshly ground black pepper

2 garlic cloves, minced

1 cup dry red wine

**Serves 4 ◦ Prep time: 10 minutes (plus 4 to 8 hours to marinate)
Cook time: 20 minutes**

For this recipe, you can use flat iron, skirt, or tri-tip (bottom sirloin) steak, all of which come in about 1- to 1½-pound cuts, so the recipe will serve four to six depending on the size. Serve it alongside your favorite starch and steamed veggie for a complete meal.

TO MAKE THE MARINADE AND STEAK

1   In a small bowl, whisk the wine, garlic, olive oil, soy sauce, thyme, and mustard. Pour into a resealable bag and add the steak. Refrigerate the steak to marinate for 4 to 8 hours. Remove the steak from the marinade and pat it dry with paper towels.

2   In a large skillet over medium-high heat, heat the olive oil until it shimmers.

3   Add the steak and cook for about 4 minutes per side until deeply browned on each side and the steak reaches an internal temperature of 140°F. Remove the steak from the skillet and put it on a plate tented with aluminum foil to keep warm, while you prepare the mushroom sauce.

4   When the mushroom sauce is ready, slice the steak against the grain into ½-inch-thick slices.

TO MAKE THE MUSHROOM SAUCE

1   In the same skillet over medium-high heat, heat the olive oil until it shimmers.

2   Add the mushrooms, sea salt, thyme, and pepper. Cook for about 6 minutes, stirring very infrequently, until the mushrooms are browned.

3   Add the garlic and cook for 30 seconds, stirring constantly.

4   Stir in the wine, and use the side of a wooden spoon to scrape and fold in any browned bits from the bottom of the skillet. Cook for about 4 minutes, stirring occasionally, until the liquid reduces by half. Serve the mushrooms spooned over the steak.

COOKING TIP: *The trick to cooking really tasty mushrooms is to leave them alone as much as possible. Let the mushrooms sit in contact with the pan for at least 2 minutes before you stir them. Stir only 2 or 3 times during the cooking process to promote browning and prevent burning. You'll know they are ready when they have released their liquid and it has evaporated, and the mushrooms are well browned on all sides.*

Per Serving Calories: 405; Protein: 33g; Total Carbohydrates: 7g; Sugars: 2g; Fiber: <1g; Total Fat: 22g; Saturated Fat: 5g; Cholesterol: 67mg; Sodium: 430mg

Greek Meatballs (Keftedes)

Serves 4 ◆ Prep time: 20 minutes ◆ Cook time: 25 minutes

2 whole-wheat
    bread slices

1¼ pounds ground
    turkey

1 egg

¼ cup seasoned
    whole-wheat
    bread crumbs

3 garlic cloves,
    minced

¼ red onion, grated

¼ cup chopped fresh
    Italian parsley
    leaves

2 tablespoons
    chopped fresh
    mint leaves

2 tablespoons
    chopped fresh
    oregano leaves

½ teaspoon sea salt

¼ teaspoon freshly
    ground black
    pepper

This comfort food from my childhood reminds me of cozy Sundays, when we'd all gather and my mom and grandma would make these meatballs for us. To this day, when my mom makes them, all her grandkids fight over who will get the last one—how's that for a testament?

1   Preheat the oven to 350°F.

2   Line a baking sheet with parchment paper or aluminum foil.

3   Run the bread under water to wet it, and squeeze out any excess. Tear the wet bread into small pieces and place it in a medium bowl.

4   Add the turkey, egg, bread crumbs, garlic, red onion, parsley, mint, oregano, sea salt, and pepper. Mix well. Form the mixture into ¼-cup-size balls. Place the meatballs on the prepared sheet and bake for about 25 minutes, or until the internal temperature reaches 165°F.

SUBSTITUTION TIP: *If you cannot find fresh herbs, substitute 1 teaspoon dried oregano and 1 teaspoon dried mint. I definitely recommend the fresh parsley, though!*

Per Serving Calories: 350; Protein: 42g; Total Carbohydrates: 10g; Sugars: 1g; Fiber: 3g; Total Fat: 18g; Saturated Fat: 3g; Cholesterol: 186mg; Sodium: 493mg

Lamb with String Beans
(Arni me Fasolakia)

DAIRY-FREE

GLUTEN-FREE

MEAL IN ONE

Serves 6 ◆ Prep time: 10 minutes ◆ Cook time: 1 hour

I remember my mom inviting me to make this dish with her. She would trim the ends off the green beans and I would help—I was so excited to be working with her! And although this calls for green beans, the ways you can vary this versatile dish are endless—see the tip for some ideas.

1　In a large skillet over medium-high heat, heat 2 tablespoons of olive oil until it shimmers.

2　Season the lamb chops with ½ teaspoon of sea salt and ⅛ teaspoon of pepper. Cook the lamb in the hot oil for about 4 minutes per side until browned on both sides. Transfer the meat to a platter and set aside.

3　Return the skillet to the heat and add the remaining 2 tablespoons of olive oil. Heat until it shimmers.

4　In a bowl, dissolve the tomato paste in the hot water. Add it to the hot skillet along with the green beans, onion, tomatoes, and the remaining ½ teaspoon of sea salt and ¼ teaspoon of pepper. Bring to a simmer, using the side of a spoon to scrape and fold in any browned bits from the bottom of the pan.

5　Return the lamb chops to the pan. Bring to a boil and reduce the heat to medium-low. Simmer for 45 minutes until the beans are soft, adding additional water as needed to adjust the thickness of the sauce.

VARIATION TIP: *I love to use okra in place of the green beans. Instead of lamb, try this dish with chicken or lean ground meat. You can also add potatoes. Peel 2 potatoes and cut them into ½-inch cubes. Add to the pot with the tomatoes and other ingredients. It's also terrific over rice or grains.*

Per Serving Calories: 439; Protein: 50g; Total Carbohydrates: 10g; Sugars: 4g; Fiber: 4g; Total Fat: 22g; Saturated Fat: 6g; Cholesterol: 153mg; Sodium: 456mg

¼ cup extra-virgin olive oil, divided

6 lamb chops, trimmed of extra fat

1 teaspoon sea salt, divided

½ teaspoon freshly ground black pepper

2 tablespoons tomato paste

1½ cups hot water

1 pound green beans, trimmed and halved crosswise

1 onion, chopped

2 tomatoes, chopped

13

Easy Vegetable Sides

EASY BRUSSELS SPROUTS HASH 182

ROASTED ASPARAGUS *with* **LEMON** *and* **PINE NUTS** 183

CITRUS SAUTÉED SPINACH 184

MASHED CAULIFLOWER 185

BROCCOLI *with* **GINGER** *and* **GARLIC** 186

BALSAMIC ROASTED CARROTS 187

PARMESAN ZUCCHINI STICKS 188

LEMON KALE *with* **SLIVERED ALMONDS** 189

ROASTED FENNEL *with* **TOMATOES** 190

GRILLED ZUCCHINI *with* **YOGURT** *and* **POMEGRANATE** 191

TOURLI GREEK BAKED VEGETABLES 192

ARTICHOKES AGINARES AL GRECO 193

Left: Grilled Zucchini with Yogurt and Pomegranate, p. 191

Easy Brussels Sprouts Hash

3 tablespoons extra-virgin olive oil

1 onion, finely chopped

1 pound Brussels sprouts, bottoms trimmed off, shredded (see tip)

½ teaspoon caraway seeds

½ teaspoon sea salt

⅛ teaspoon freshly ground black pepper

¼ cup red wine vinegar

1 tablespoon Dijon mustard

1 tablespoon honey

3 garlic cloves, minced

Serves 4 ◆ Prep time: 10 minutes ◆ Cook time: 20 minutes

Cutting Brussels sprouts into small pieces makes them cook quite quickly in this delicious side dish for meat, poultry, or fish. This is a great "intro" to Brussels sprouts for people who don't think they like them.

1   In a large skillet over medium-high heat, heat the olive oil until it shimmers.

2   Add the onion, Brussels sprouts, caraway seeds, sea salt, and pepper. Cook for 7 to 10 minutes, stirring occasionally, until the Brussels sprouts begin to brown.

3   While the Brussels sprouts cook, whisk the vinegar, mustard, and honey in a small bowl and set aside.

4   Add the garlic to the skillet and cook for 30 seconds, stirring constantly.

5   Add the vinegar mixture to the skillet. Cook for about 5 minutes, stirring, until the liquid reduces by half.

COOKING TIP: *An easy way to prepare the sprouts is to carefully grate them on a box grater, or use a mandoline set at ¼ inch with a guard. It allows you to have pieces of similar size so they cook evenly.*

Per Serving Calories: 176; Protein: 11g; Total Carbohydrates: 19g; Sugars: 8g; Fiber: 5g; Total Fat: 11g; Saturated Fat: 1g; Cholesterol: 0mg; Sodium: 309mg

Roasted Asparagus with Lemon and Pine Nuts

DAIRY-FREE
GLUTEN-FREE
UNDER 30 MINUTES
VEGAN

Serves 4 • Prep time: 5 minutes • Cook time: 20 minutes

Roasting anything makes it special. Asparagus is no exception, as this cooking method turns the ends crisp and gives them a tasty crunch. Roasting also adds deep caramelization, which adds a lot of flavor to this easy side dish.

1   Preheat the oven to 425°F.

2   In a large bowl, toss the asparagus with the olive oil, lemon juice and zest, pine nuts, sea salt, and pepper. Spread in a roasting pan in an even layer.

3   Roast for about 20 minutes until the asparagus is browned.

COOKING TIP: *To trim asparagus quickly, hold each end of a spear (about an inch from the ends) between two fingers and bend until it snaps. Discard the woody end.*

Per Serving Calories: 144; Protein: 4g; Total Carbohydrates: 6g; Sugars: 3g; Fiber: 3g; Total Fat: 13g; Saturated Fat: 1g; Cholesterol: 0mg; Sodium: 240mg

1 pound asparagus, trimmed

2 tablespoons extra-virgin olive oil

Juice of 1 lemon

Zest of 1 lemon

¼ cup pine nuts

½ teaspoon sea salt

⅛ teaspoon freshly ground black pepper

Citrus Sautéed Spinach

DAIRY-FREE

GLUTEN-FREE

UNDER 30 MINUTES

VEGAN

2 tablespoons extra-
    virgin olive oil

4 cups fresh baby
    spinach

1 teaspoon orange
    zest

¼ cup freshly
    squeezed orange
    juice

½ teaspoon sea salt

⅛ teaspoon freshly
    ground black
    pepper

Serves 4 ◆ Prep time: 5 minutes ◆ Cook time: 5 minutes

Spinach and citrus have a natural affinity for one another—the two flavors meld nicely. While you can use any citrus that appeals to you (try grapefruit!), this version is made with freshly squeezed orange juice and zest.

1   In a large skillet over medium-high heat, heat the olive oil until it shimmers.

2   Add the spinach and orange zest. Cook for about 3 minutes, stirring occasionally, until the spinach wilts.

3   Stir in the orange juice, sea salt, and pepper. Cook for 2 minutes more, stirring occasionally. Serve hot.

VARIATION TIP: *Before serving, add ¼ cup chopped walnuts for crunch. The recipe also works with kale or Swiss chard, but increase the cooking time to about 10 minutes.*

Per Serving Calories: 74; Protein: 7g; Total Carbohydrates: 3g; Sugars: 1g; Fiber: <1g; Total Fat: 7g; Saturated Fat: <1g; Cholesterol: 0mg; Sodium: 258mg

Mashed Cauliflower

Serves 4 • Prep time: 10 minutes • Cook time: 15 minutes

GLUTEN-FREE
UNDER 30 MINUTES
VEGAN

Mashed cauliflower makes a great alternative to mashed potatoes that's lower in calories and carbs. It also has lots of vitamins C, K, B_6, and folate. This version will keep well for about three days in the refrigerator, so you can make it ahead.

1   In a large pot over medium-high, cover the cauliflower with water and bring it to a boil. Reduce the heat to medium-low, cover, and simmer for about 10 minutes until the cauliflower is soft.

2   Drain the cauliflower and return it to the pot. Add the milk, cheese, butter, olive oil, sea salt, and pepper. Using a potato masher, mash until smooth.

SUBSTITUTION TIPS: *If you substitute olive oil for the butter, you'll eliminate the saturated fat and cholesterol and lower the calorie count. To make this dairy free, omit the milk, cheese, and butter. Replace the milk with almond milk, and increase the olive oil to 3 tablespoons. Add 6 roasted garlic cloves before mashing the cauliflower. Roast whole heads of garlic at 350°F wrapped in aluminum foil for 1 hour.*

Per Serving Calories: 187; Protein: 7g; Total Carbohydrates: 7g; Sugars: 3g; Fiber: 3g; Total Fat: 16g; Saturated Fat: 7g; Cholesterol: 26mg; Sodium: 445mg

4 cups cauliflower florets

¼ cup skim milk

¼ cup (2 ounces) grated Parmesan cheese

2 tablespoons butter

2 tablespoons extra-virgin olive oil

½ teaspoon sea salt

⅛ teaspoon freshly ground black pepper

Broccoli with Ginger and Garlic

Serves 4 ◦ Prep time: 10 minutes ◦ Cook time: 11 minutes

2 tablespoons extra-
   virgin olive oil

2 cups broccoli
   florets

1 tablespoon grated
   fresh ginger

½ teaspoon sea salt

⅛ teaspoon freshly
   ground black
   pepper

3 garlic cloves,
   minced

Stir-frying broccoli allows you to cook it to that perfect consistency of crisp-tender. The ginger and garlic are elegant flavor complements to the broccoli. This makes an excellent side dish for meat or poultry.

1   In a large skillet over medium-high heat, heat the olive oil until
    it shimmers.

2   Add the broccoli, ginger, sea salt, and pepper. Cook for about
    10 minutes, stirring occasionally, until the broccoli is soft and starts
    to brown.

3   Add the garlic and cook for 30 seconds, stirring constantly. Remove
    from the heat and serve.

COOKING TIP: *When cooking garlic, it can burn quickly and impart bitter flavors. That's why adding it toward the end of cooking in olive oil, and cooking for only 30 seconds while stirring constantly, are so important. The stirring keeps the garlic from burning, while cooking it for just 30 seconds allows it to release its fragrance and flavors without overcooking.*

Per Serving Calories: 80; Protein: 1g; Total Carbohydrates: 4g; Sugars: <1g; Fiber: 1g; Total Fat: 0g; Saturated Fat: <1g; Cholesterol: 0mg; Sodium: 249mg

Balsamic Roasted Carrots

DAIRY-FREE

GLUTEN-FREE

VEGAN

Serves 4 ◆ **Prep time: 10 minutes** ◆ **Cook time: 30 minutes**

Roasting carrots (and other root vegetables) imparts a deep, caramelized flavor that makes them hearty and satisfying. The divine flavor is elevated even further with the addition of balsamic vinegar. Choose a balsamic vinegar with a flavor you like by itself for best results.

1 Preheat the oven to 425°F.

2 In a large bowl, toss the carrots with the olive oil, sea salt, and pepper. Place in a single layer in a roasting pan or on a rimmed baking sheet. Roast for 20 to 30 minutes until the carrots are caramelized.

3 Toss with the vinegar and serve.

VARIATION TIP: *Try this recipe with parsnips or turnips.*

Per Serving Calories: 132; Protein: 1g; Total Carbohydrates: 17g; Sugars: 8g; Fiber: 4g; Total Fat: 7g; Saturated Fat: <1g; Cholesterol: 0mg; Sodium: 235mg

1½ pounds carrots, quartered lengthwise

2 tablespoons extra-virgin olive oil

¼ teaspoon sea salt

⅛ teaspoon freshly ground black pepper

3 tablespoons balsamic vinegar

Parmesan Zucchini Sticks

Serves 4 ◆ **Prep time: 10 minutes** ◆ **Cook time: 20 minutes**

4 zucchini, quartered lengthwise

2 tablespoons extra-virgin olive oil

½ cup (4 ounces) grated Parmesan cheese

1 tablespoon Italian seasoning

½ teaspoon sea salt

¼ teaspoon garlic powder

⅛ teaspoon freshly ground black pepper

These tempting zucchini sticks make a great alternative to French fries. The Parmesan and herb coating crisps in just a minute or two under the broiler after roasting. Serve as a veggie side dish or as a snack for dipping in marinara sauce or pesto.

1 Preheat the oven to 350°F.

2 In a large bowl, toss the zucchini with the olive oil.

3 In a small bowl, whisk the cheese, Italian seasoning, sea salt, garlic powder, and pepper. Toss with the zucchini.

4 Place the zucchini in a single layer on a rimmed baking sheet. Bake for 15 to 20 minutes until the zucchini is soft.

5 Set the oven to broil, and broil for 1 to 2 minutes until the cheese-herb coating crisps, watching carefully so it doesn't burn.

SUBSTITUTION TIP: *To make this dairy free, replace the Parmesan cheese with ½ cup nutritional yeast.*

Per Serving Calories: 194; Protein: 12g; Total Carbohydrates: 8g; Sugars: 4g; Fiber: 2g; Total Fat: 14g; Saturated Fat: 5g; Cholesterol: 0mg; Sodium: 235mg

Lemon Kale with Slivered Almonds

GLUTEN-FREE
UNDER 30 MINUTES
VEGAN

Serves 4 ◆ Prep time: 10 minutes ◆ Cook time: 15 minutes

Kale is a nutritional powerhouse, and adding a little lemon boosts the flavor while the almonds add crunch and protein. This recipe also works with other types of greens, including Swiss chard and mustard greens.

1 In a large skillet over medium-high heat, heat the olive oil until it shimmers.

2 Add the kale, sea salt, and pepper. Cook for 7 to 10 minutes, stirring occasionally, until soft.

3 Add the lemon juice and zest and the almonds. Cook for about 3 minutes more, stirring occasionally, until the liquid reduces by half. Serve immediately.

SUBSTITUTION TIP: *Walnuts make a good substitution for the almonds. If you're allergic to tree nuts, add ¼ cup sunflower seeds instead.*

Per Serving Calories: 131; Protein: 3g; Total Carbohydrates: 9g; Sugars: <1g; Fiber: 2g; Total Fat: 10g; Saturated Fat: 1g; Cholesterol: 0mg; Sodium: 266mg

2 tablespoons extra-virgin olive oil

4 cups chopped stemmed kale

½ teaspoon sea salt

⅛ teaspoon freshly ground black pepper

Juice of 1 lemon

Zest of 1 lemon

¼ cup slivered almonds

Roasted Fennel with Tomatoes

Serves 4 ◆ **Prep time: 10 minutes** ◆ **Cook time: 25 minutes**

2 fennel bulbs, cored
  and cut into
  ½-inch-thick
  pieces

20 cherry tomatoes,
  halved

¼ cup extra-virgin
  olive oil

½ teaspoon sea salt

¼ teaspoon freshly
  ground black
  pepper

Fennel has a light anise flavor that deepens with the caramelization
of roasting. The acidity of the cherry tomatoes serves as a distinctive
counterpoint to the fennel, and the result is a fragrant and flavorful
vegetable side dish.

1   Preheat the oven to 425°F.

2   In a large bowl, toss the fennel and tomatoes with the olive oil, sea salt,
     and pepper. Spread in an even layer in a roasting pan or on a rimmed
     baking sheet. Roast for 20 to 25 minutes until the fennel is soft and
     browned. Serve hot.

VARIATION TIP: *Add ¼ cup pine nuts to the vegetables before roasting.*

Per Serving Calories: 237; Protein: 7g; Total Carbohydrates: 33g; Sugars: 16g; Fiber: 11g; Total Fat: 12g;
Saturated Fat: 1g; Cholesterol: 0mg; Sodium: 325mg

Grilled Zucchini with Yogurt and Pomegranate

GLUTEN-FREE

UNDER 30 MINUTES

VEGETARIAN

Serves 4 • Prep time: 10 minutes • Cook time: 6 minutes

Grilling vegetables gives them a smoky flavor that's really transformative from their raw origins. If you don't have an outdoor grill, use a grill pan or an indoor electric grill.

1   Preheat the grill to high heat.

2   Brush the zucchini pieces on both sides with olive oil and sprinkle with ½ teaspoon of sea salt. Grill for about 3 minutes per side until soft and starting to brown. Arrange on a platter.

3   In a small bowl, whisk the yogurt, chili powder, and remaining ¼ teaspoon of sea salt. Drizzle over the zucchini. Sprinkle with the pomegranate seeds.

INGREDIENT TIP: *To remove seeds (arils) from a pomegranate, cut it in half and hold it, cut-side down, over a bowl or plate. Firmly tap the pomegranate shell with a wooden spoon.*

Per Serving Calories: 154; Protein: 8g; Total Carbohydrates: 20g; Sugars: 11g; Fiber: 3g; Total Fat: 8g; Saturated Fat: 1g; Cholesterol: 1mg; Sodium: 388mg

4 zucchini, sliced

2 tablespoons extra-virgin olive oil

¾ teaspoon sea salt, divided

¼ cup unsweetened nonfat plain Greek yogurt

1 teaspoon chili powder

¼ cup pomegranate seeds

Tourli Greek Baked Vegetables

Serves 8 ◆ Prep time: 20 minutes ◆ Cook time: 2 hours

**Nonstick cooking
spray**

**2 tablespoons extra-
virgin olive oil**

**1½ tablespoons
tomato paste**

**1½ tablespoons
water**

Juice of 1 lemon

**3 tablespoons
chopped
fresh Italian
parsley leaves**

½ teaspoons sea salt

**¼ teaspoon freshly
ground black
pepper**

2 onions, sliced

2 carrots, sliced

2 tomatoes, chopped

1 eggplant, sliced

**1 cup green beans,
ends removed**

1 potato, sliced

**1 red bell pepper,
sliced**

**1 yellow squash,
sliced**

1 zucchini, sliced

The aroma of this dish as it cooks is intoxicating—and, for me, it's
a really fresh, warm comfort food reminiscent of my childhood. My
sisters and I couldn't resist picking off the eggplant layer before the
dish was even served—despite my mother's pleadings. If you're lucky
enough to have any left, they make excellent leftovers.

1 Preheat the oven to 375°F. Spray a 9-by-13-inch casserole dish with
   nonstick cooking spray.

2 In a large bowl, whisk the olive oil, tomato paste, water, lemon juice,
   parsley, sea salt, and pepper.

3 Add the onions, carrots, tomatoes, eggplant, green beans, potato,
   red bell pepper, squash, and zucchini and toss to coat. Transfer to the
   prepared dish. Cover with aluminum foil and bake for 1 hour. Serve hot.

COOKING TIP: *Add any vegetables you like here. They cook down,
so to make 1 cup baked vegetables, you'll need 2 cups raw vegetables.*

Per Serving Calories: 110; Protein: 3g; Total Carbohydrates: 19g; Sugars: 10g; Fiber: 5g; Total Fat: 4g;
Saturated Fat: <1g; Cholesterol: 0mg; Sodium: 142mg

Artichokes Aginares al Greco

DAIRY-FREE
GLUTEN-FREE
MEAL IN ONE
VEGAN

Serves 4 • Prep time: 10 minutes • Cook time: 40 minutes

My mom makes this for every holiday. It's so good that every time somebody new tries it, they ask her for the recipe. This can be enjoyed all by itself or alongside fish or meat.

1 In a large pot over medium-high heat, heat 2 tablespoons of olive oil until it shimmers.

2 Add the onion, carrots, and celery. Cook for 5 to 10 minutes, stirring occasionally, until the vegetables are tender.

3 Add the lemon juice, water, and the remaining 2 tablespoons of olive oil. Bring to a boil. Reduce the heat to medium-low and simmer for about 15 minutes until the carrots are tender, adding more water as needed.

4 Add the artichoke hearts, dill, sea salt, and pepper. Cover and cook for 10 minutes more until the artichokes are tender.

5 Stir in the peas just before serving.

SUBSTITUTION TIP: *If you don't have fresh dill, substitute 2 teaspoons dried dill.*

Per Serving Calories: 273; Protein: 9g; Total Carbohydrates: 33g; Sugars: 7g; Fiber: 15g; Total Fat: 15g; Saturated Fat: 2g; Cholesterol: 0mg; Sodium: 471mg

¼ cup extra-virgin olive oil, divided

1 cup sliced onion

12 whole baby carrots

½ cup chopped celery

Juice of 1 lemon

¾ cup water

10 frozen artichoke hearts, halved

¼ cup chopped fresh dill

½ teaspoon sea salt

⅛ teaspoon freshly ground black pepper

¾ cup peas

14

Sweets

LEMON *and* WATERMELON GRANITA   196

BAKED APPLES *with* WALNUTS *and* SPICES   197

RED WINE POACHED PEARS   198

VANILLA PUDDING *with* STRAWBERRIES   199

MIXED BERRY FROZEN YOGURT BAR   200

FRUIT SALAD *with* YOGURT CREAM   201

DATE NUT ENERGY BALLS   202

PASTAFLORA   203

Left: Date Nut Energy Balls, p. 202

Lemon and Watermelon Granita

4 cups watermelon cubes

¼ cup honey

¼ cup freshly squeezed lemon juice

Serves 4 • Prep time: 10 minutes (plus 3 hours to freeze) • Cook time: None

Making a granita doesn't take a lot of active time, but it does require you to rough it up with a fork every so often while it's in the freezer to keep it fluffy and icy. The result is a refreshing frozen dessert.

1   In a blender, combine the watermelon, honey, and lemon juice. Purée all the ingredients, then pour into a 9-by-9-by-2-inch baking pan and place in the freezer.

2   Every 30 to 60 minutes, run a fork across the frozen surface to fluff and create ice flakes. Freeze for about 3 hours total and serve.

LEFTOVERS TIP: *Serve leftovers like Italian ice, scraping it into cups with a spoon, or give it a quick pulse in a food processor or blender to fluff it back up.*

VARIATION TIP: *Using the proportions above, try watermelon and lime juice, cantaloupe and lime juice, or honeydew and orange juice for other refreshing flavor variations.*

Per Serving Calories: 153; Protein: 2g; Total Carbohydrates: 39g; Sugars: 35g; Fiber: 1g; Total Fat: <1g; Saturated Fat: <1g; Cholesterol: 0mg; Sodium: 7mg

Baked Apples with Walnuts and Spices

DAIRY-FREE
GLUTEN-FREE
VEGETARIAN

Serves 4 ◆ **Prep time: 10 minutes** ◆ **Cook time: 45 minutes**

Using fruit as the basis of a dessert is part of what makes the Mediterranean diet so nutritious—and so successful. These baked apples make a warm, fragrant, and satisfying dessert that is the perfect finish for any meal.

1 Preheat the oven to 375°F.

2 Cut the tops off the apples and use a metal spoon or paring knife to remove the cores, leaving the bottoms of the apples intact. Place the apples cut-side up in a 9-by-9-inch baking pan.

3 In a small bowl, stir together the walnuts, honey, cinnamon, nutmeg, ginger, and sea salt. Spoon the mixture into the centers of the apples. Bake the apples for about 45 minutes until browned, soft, and fragrant. Serve warm.

SUBSTITUTION TIP: *To make these vegan, replace the honey with ¼ cup packed brown sugar. To make them nut free, replace the walnuts with ¼ cup flaxseed meal.*

Per Serving Calories: 199; Protein: 5g; Total Carbohydrates: 41g; Sugars: 32g; Fiber: 6g; Total Fat: 5g; Saturated Fat: <1g; Cholesterol: 0mg; Sodium: 41mg

4 apples
¼ cup chopped
walnuts
2 tablespoons honey
1 teaspoon ground
cinnamon
¼ teaspoon ground
nutmeg
¼ teaspoon ground
ginger
Pinch sea salt

Red Wine Poached Pears

Serves 4 • Prep time: 10 minutes • Cook time: 45 minutes (plus 3 hours to chill)

2 cups dry red wine

¼ cup honey

Zest of ½ orange

2 cinnamon sticks

1 (1-inch) piece fresh
   ginger

4 pears, bottom inch
   sliced off so the
   pear is flat

Poaching pears in red wine gives them a beautiful ruby color that makes this a showpiece dessert, ideal for serving guests or just enjoying yourselves. Because of the long cooking and chilling time, this may be a better weekend dessert, when things are, hopefully, less hurried.

1   In a large pot over medium-high heat, stir together the wine, honey, orange zest, cinnamon, and ginger. Bring to a boil, stirring occasionally. Reduce the heat to medium-low and simmer for 5 minutes to let the flavors blend.

2   Add the pears to the pot. Cover and simmer for 20 minutes until the pears are tender, turning every 3 to 4 minutes to ensure even color and contact with the liquid. Refrigerate the pears in the liquid for 3 hours to allow for more flavor absorption.

3   Bring the pears and liquid to room temperature. Place the pears on individual dishes and return the poaching liquid to the stove top over medium-high heat. Simmer for 15 minutes until the liquid is syrupy. Serve the pears with the liquid drizzled over the top.

SUBSTITUTION TIP: *You can also poach the pears in a sweet wine. Use 2 cups sweet dessert wine, such as ice wine or Sauternes. Use the same spices; just omit the honey.*

Per Serving Calories: 283; Protein: <1g; Total Carbohydrates: 53g; Sugars: 39g; Fiber: 7g; Total Fat: <1g; Saturated Fat: 0g; Cholesterol: 0mg; Sodium: 9mg

Vanilla Pudding with Strawberries

Serves 4 • Prep time: 10 minutes • Cook time: 10 minutes (plus chilling time)

Rediscover pudding! Homemade pudding is so much more flavorful than the stuff that comes in a box, and it really doesn't take much longer to make. The longest part is waiting for the pudding to chill, which takes about an hour.

1   In a small bowl, whisk 2 cups of milk with the egg, sugar, vanilla, and sea salt. Transfer the mixture to a medium pot, place it over medium heat, and slowly bring to a boil, whisking constantly.

2   In a small bowl, whisk the cornstarch with the remaining ¼ cup of milk. In a thin stream, whisk this slurry into the boiling mixture in the pot. Cook until it thickens, stirring constantly. Boil for 1 minute more, stirring constantly.

3   Spoon the pudding into 4 dishes and refrigerate to chill. Serve topped with the sliced strawberries.

VARIATION TIP: *Wild blackberries, which are in season in late summer, make a great substitute for the strawberries. If you have a patch growing nearby, pick them and enjoy a late-summer treat.*

SUBSTITUTION TIP: *To make this dairy free, substitute almond milk for the skim milk.*

Per Serving Calories: 209; Protein: 6g; Total Carbohydrates: 43g; Sugars: 36g; Fiber: 2g; Total Fat: 1g; Saturated Fat: <1g; Cholesterol: 44mg; Sodium: 129mg

2¼ cups skim milk, divided

1 egg, beaten

½ cup sugar

1 teaspoon vanilla extract

Pinch sea salt

3 tablespoons cornstarch

2 cups sliced strawberries

Mixed Berry Frozen Yogurt Bar

Serves 8 • Prep time: 10 minutes • Cook time: None

8 cups low-fat vanilla frozen yogurt (or flavor of choice)

1 cup sliced fresh strawberries

1 cup fresh blueberries

1 cup fresh blackberries

1 cup fresh raspberries

½ cup chopped walnuts

When you're entertaining, a frozen yogurt bar is a great way to present a fun dessert that is still nutritious and flavorful. The berries listed are just suggestions. Add your favorite fruits and berries—whatever is in season—for this easy dessert.

Apportion the yogurt among 8 dessert bowls. Serve the toppings family style, and let your guests choose their toppings and spoon them over the yogurt.

VARIATION TIP: *Other fruits that work well with a yogurt bar include chopped melon, such as honeydew or cantaloupe, chopped pears or apples, chopped plums, or dried fruits, such as dried cranberries or currants.*

Per Serving Calories: 81; Protein: 3g; Total Carbohydrates: 9g; Sugars: 5g; Fiber: 3g; Total Fat: 5g; Saturated Fat: <1g; Cholesterol: 0mg; Sodium: 1mg

Fruit Salad with Yogurt Cream

Serves 4 • Prep time: 10 minutes • Cook time: None

GLUTEN-FREE

UNDER 30 MINUTES

VEGETARIAN

When making fruit salad, you get the most flavor if you choose what's seasonally available. That said, feel free to customize this salad using whatever is in season and adding about 4 cups fruit in total.

1   In a large bowl, combine the grapes, cantaloupe, plums, peach, and blueberries. Toss to mix. Divide among 4 dessert dishes.

2   In a small bowl, whisk the yogurt, honey, and cinnamon. Spoon over the fruit.

VARIATION TIP: *For a little crunch, top each serving with 2 tablespoons chopped pecans.*

Per Serving Calories: 159; Protein: 3g; Total Carbohydrates: 38g; Sugars: 33g; Fiber: 2g; Total Fat: <1g; Saturated Fat: <1g; Cholesterol: 2mg; Sodium: 33mg

1½ cups grapes, halved

1 cup chopped cantaloupe

2 plums, chopped

1 peach, chopped

½ cup fresh blueberries

1 cup unsweetened plain nonfat Greek yogurt

2 tablespoons honey

½ teaspoon ground cinnamon

Date Nut Energy Balls

Serves 24 • **Prep time: 10 minutes** • **Cook time: None**

1 cup walnuts

1 cup almonds

2 cups Medjool
dates, pitted

2 tablespoons extra-
virgin olive oil

¼ cup unsweetened
cocoa powder

¼ cup shredded
unsweetened
coconut, plus
additional for
coating

Pinch sea salt

These energy balls make a tasty dessert, and they freeze well for when
you need a snack on the go. Dates add sweetness without added sugar.
A serving size is one ball and provides natural sustained energy when
you need a boost.

1 In a blender or food processor, combine the walnuts, almonds,
    dates, olive oil, cocoa powder, coconut, and sea salt. Pulse for
    20 to 30 (1-second pulses) until everything is well chopped. Form
    the mixture into 24 balls.

2 Spread the additional coconut on a plate and roll the balls in the
    coconut to coat. Serve, refrigerate, or freeze.

VARIATION TIP: *If you're allergic to tree nuts, substitute 1 cup peanuts
and 1 cup sunflower seeds for the walnuts and almonds.*

Per Serving Calories: 164; Protein: 3g; Total Carbohydrates: 26g; Sugars: 20g; Fiber: 3g; Total Fat: 6g;
Saturated Fat: 1g; Cholesterol: 0mg; Sodium: 19mg

Pastaflora

Serves 24 ◆ **Prep time: 15 minutes** ◆ **Cook time: 35 minutes**

This is not a common dish, but my mom makes this; in fact, she makes it so well, a big company once asked her to sell the recipe. She declined, but she does make extra for her friends and family. You may want to follow her lead and make two batches—one to enjoy and the other to send home with your appreciative guests.

1   Preheat the oven to 400°F.

2   Coat a 9-by-13-inch baking dish with cooking spray.

3   In a food processor, combine the flour, sugar, vanilla, butter, baking powder, eggs, and orange zest. Pulse until a stiff dough forms. Press three-fourths of the dough into the prepared dish.

4   Spread the jam over the dough.

5   Roll out the remaining dough to ¼-inch thickness and cut it into ½-inch-wide strips. Form a lattice over the top of the jam with the strips. Bake for about 35 minutes until golden. Cool on a wire rack.

6   Cut into 24 cookies and serve.

VARIATION TIP: *Use any flavor jam or preserves here. Try strawberry or blackberry jam. (For the record, we've tried them all—we keep coming back to apricot!)*

Per Serving Calories: 102; Protein: 2g; Total Carbohydrates: 15g; Sugars: 6g; Fiber: <1g; Total Fat: 4g; Saturated Fat: 3g; Cholesterol: 24mg; Sodium: 34mg

Nonstick cooking spray

2 cups all-purpose flour

½ cup sugar

1 teaspoon vanilla extract

½ cup (1 stick) unsalted butter

2 teaspoons baking powder

2 eggs

2 tablespoons orange zest

¼ cup apricot jam

Measurement Conversions

◇◇

Volume Equivalents (Dry)

US STANDARD	METRIC (APPROXIMATE)
⅛ teaspoon	0.5 mL
¼ teaspoon	1 mL
½ teaspoon	2 mL
¾ teaspoon	4 mL
1 teaspoon	5 mL
1 tablespoon	15 mL
¼ cup	59 mL
⅓ cup	79 mL
½ cup	118 mL
⅔ cup	156 mL
¾ cup	177 mL
1 cup	235 mL
2 cups or 1 pint	475 mL
3 cups	700 mL
4 cups or 1 quart	1 L
½ gallon	2 L
1 gallon	4 L

Volume Equivalents (Liquid)

US STANDARD	US STANDARD (OUNCES)	METRIC (APPROXIMATE)
2 tablespoons	1 fl. oz.	30 mL
¼ cup	2 fl. oz.	60 mL
½ cup	4 fl. oz.	120 mL
1 cup	8 fl. oz.	240 mL
1½ cups	12 fl. oz.	355 mL
2 cups or 1 pint	16 fl. oz.	475 mL
4 cups or 1 quart	32 fl. oz.	1 L
1 gallon	128 fl. oz.	4 L

Oven Temperatures

FAHRENHEIT (F)	CELSIUS (C) (APPROXIMATE)
250°F	120°C
300°F	150°C
325°F	165°C
350°F	180°C
375°F	190°C
400°F	200°C
425°F	220°C
450°F	230°C

Weight Equivalents

US STANDARD	METRIC (APPROXIMATE)
½ ounce	15 g
1 ounce	30 g
2 ounces	60 g
4 ounces	115 g
8 ounces	225 g
12 ounces	340 g
16 ounces or 1 pound	455 g

The Dirty Dozen and the Clean Fifteen

A nonprofit and environmental organization called Environmental Working Group (EWG) looks at data supplied by the US Department of Agriculture (USDA) and the Food and Drug Administration (FDA) about pesticide residues and compiles a list each year of the best and worst pesticide loads found in commercial crops. The Dirty Dozen list advises which fruits and vegetables you should always buy organic. The Clean Fifteen list lets you know which produce is considered safe enough, when grown conventionally, to allow you to skip the organics. This does not mean that the Clean Fifteen produce is pesticide-free, though, so wash these fruits and vegetables thoroughly.

These lists change every year, so make sure you look up the most recent before you fill your shopping cart. You'll find the most recent lists as well as a guide to pesticides in produce at EWG.org/FoodNews.

2017 Dirty Dozen

Apples	Spinach
Celery	Strawberries
Cherry tomatoes	Sweet bell peppers
Cucumbers	*In addition to the Dirty Dozen, the EWG added two foods contaminated with highly toxic organophosphate insecticides:*
Grapes	
Nectarines	
Peaches	
Potatoes	
Snap peas	Hot peppers
	Kale/Collard greens

2017 Clean Fifteen

Asparagus	Onions
Avocados	Papayas
Cabbage	Pineapples
Cantaloupe	Sweet corn
Cauliflower	Sweet peas (frozen)
Eggplant	Sweet potatoes
Grapefruit	
Kiwis	
Mangoes	

Resources

Amazon (Amazon.com) Comprehensive online resource for cooking tools, food, and more.

American Heart Association (Heart.org) Nonprofit organization dedicated to education, research, and prevention of heart-related diseases. Comprehensive website includes weight-loss information, a BMI calculator, lifestyle recommendations, and more.

Environmental Working Group Food Scores (ewg.org/foodscores) Online tool to check the health scores of thousands of foods and food products based on their ingredients, nutrition, and processing concerns.

Exercise.com Online resource dedicated to exercises.

Mayo Clinic (Mayoclinic.org) Nonprofit health care system of resources, including articles on the Mediterranean diet, weight loss, and more.

Olive Nation (Olivenation.com) Online food shopping resource offering Mediterranean and other specialties.

Webmd.com Comprehensive health website, including articles on the benefits of the Mediterranean diet, weight loss, and more.

Yoffielife.com Expert-run wellness website, including articles on yoga, fitness, produce and grains, nutrition, weight management, and more.

References

American Heart Association. "American Heart Association Recommendations for Physical Activity in Adults." Accessed May 19, 2017. www.heart .org/HEARTORG/HealthyLiving/PhysicalActivity/FitnessBasics /American-Heart-Association-Recommendations-for-Physical-Activity -in-Adults_UCM_307976_Article.jsp#.WROL2kr3arV.

American Heart Association. "Mediterranean Diet with Virgin Olive Oil May Be Recipe for 'Good' Cholesterol." Accessed May 19, 2017. news .heart.org/mediterranean-diet-with-virgin-olive-oil-may-be-recipe-for -good-cholesterol.

American Heart Association. "Mediterranean-Style Diet Details." Accessed May 19, 2017. www.heart.org/HEARTORG/Affiliate/Mediterranean-style -diet-details_UCM_461758_Article.jsp#.WROPbUr3arU.

BMI Calculator. "Harris Benedict Equation." Accessed May 19, 2017. www.bmi-calculator.net/bmr-calculator/harris-benedict-equation.

Centers for Disease Control and Prevention. "Overweight & Obesity." Accessed May 19, 2017. www.cdc.gov/obesity.

Consumer Health Digest. "7 Healthiest Weight Loss Drinks That Really Work." Accessed May 19, 2017. www.consumerhealthdigest.com /weight-loss/7-healthiest-weight-loss-drinks.html.

Godman, Heidi. "Adopt a Mediterranean Diet Now for Better Health Later." Harvard Health Blog. Accessed May 19, 2017. www.health.harvard.edu /blog/adopt-a-mediterranean-diet-now-for-better-health-later -201311066846.

Gunnars, Kris, BSc. "5 Studies on the Mediterranean Diet—Does It Really Work?" Authority Nutrition. Accessed May 19, 2017. authoritynutrition .com/5-studies-on-the-mediterranean-diet.

Johns Hopkins Water Institute. "Water and Health." Accessed May 19, 2017. water.jhu.edu/index.php/about/water-health.

Mayo Clinic. "Mediterranean Diet: A Heart-Healthy Eating Plan." Accessed May 19, 2017. www.mayoclinic.org/healthy-lifestyle/nutrition-and -healthy-eating/in-depth/mediterranean-diet/art-20047801.

Mayo Clinic. "Water: How Much Should You Drink Every Day?" Accessed May 19, 2017. www.mayoclinic.org/healthy-lifestyle/nutrition-and -healthy-eating/in-depth/water/art-20044256.

Medline Plus, U.S. National Library of Medicine. "Obesity." Accessed May 19, 2017. medlineplus.gov/obesity.html.

Miller, Sara G. "Will Staying Hydrated Help with Weight Loss?" Live Science. Accessed May 19, 2017. www.livescience.com/55360 -water-intake-weight-obesity.html.

Mozes, Alan. "Obesity May Be Bad for the Brain, Too." *U.S. News & World Report*. Accessed May 19, 2017. health.usnews.com/health-care/articles /2016-08-10/obesity-may-be-bad-for-the-brain-too.

National Heart, Lung, and Blood Institute. "BMI Tools." Accessed May 19, 2017. www.nhlbi.nih.gov/health/educational/lose _wt/bmitools.htm.

Nutrition.gov. "Overweight and Obesity." Accessed May 19, 2017. www.nutrition.gov/nutrition-and-health-issues/overweight-and-obesity.

Oaklander, Mandy. "Weight Loss and Water Consumption Appear to Be Linked." *Time*. Accessed May 19, 2017. time.com/4403276/drink -water-hydration-weight-loss.

Shute, Nancy. "Does Putting on a Few Pounds Help You Cheat Death?" NPR. Accessed May 19, 2017. www.npr.org/sections/health-shots /2016/05/10/477376914/does-putting-on-a-few-pounds-help-you -cheat-death.

US Department of Agriculture. "Obesity Overview." Accessed May 19, 2017. www.ers.usda.gov/topics/food-choices-health/obesity.

U.S. News & World Report. "Mediterranean Diet." Accessed May 19, 2017. health.usnews.com/best-diet/mediterranean-diet.

World Health Organization. "Obesity." Accessed May 19, 2017. www.who .int/topics/obesity/en.

World Health Organization. "Physical Activity and Adults." Accessed May 19, 2017. www.who.int/dietphysicalactivity/factsheet_adults/en.

Recipe Index

A

Almond and Maple Quick
  Grits, 91
Artichokes Aginares al
  Greco, 193

B

Baba Ganoush, 101
Baked Apples with Walnuts
  and Spices, 197
Baked Gigante Beans, 143
Baked Stuffed Portobello
  Mushrooms, 141
Balsamic Roasted Carrots, 187
Berry and Yogurt Parfait, 89
Broccoli with Ginger and
  Garlic, 186
Butternut Squash Soup, 117

C

Caprese Salad, 112
Carrot and Bran Mini
  Muffins, 93
Chicken and Vegetable
  Soup, 120
Chicken with Potatoes, Figs
  and Carrots, 172
Chicken Gyros with
  Tzatziki, 173
Chicken Kapama, 169
Chicken Piccata, 167
Chicken Sausage and
  Peppers, 166
Chickpea Salad, 113
Chocolate Banana
  Smoothie, 87
Chop Chop Salad, 114
Cioppino, 159
Citrus Sautéed Spinach, 184
Crab Cakes with Shaved
  Fennel Salad, 157

Cucumber Salad, 111

D

Date Nut Energy Balls, 202
Dijon and Herb Pork
  Tenderloin, 175

E

Easy Brussels Sprouts
  Hash, 182
Easy Trail Mix, 107
Easy Zucchini Lasagna
  Wraps, 147

F

Falafel Patties, 142
Farro with Artichoke
  Hearts, 124
Flatbread with Olive
  Tapenade, 137
French Toast, 94
Fruit Salad with Yogurt
  Cream, 201
Fruit Smoothie, 88

G

Greek Meatballs, 178
Greek Salad, 110
Grilled Zucchini with Yogurt
  and Pomegranate, 191

H

Halibut en Papillote with
  Capers, Onions, Olives,
  and Tomatoes, 160
Herb-Roasted Turkey
  Breast, 165
Hummus, 100

J

Julene's Green Juice, 86

L

Lamb with String Beans, 179
Lemon and Watermelon
  Granita, 196
Lemon Kale with Slivered
  Almonds, 189
Lentil Soup, 119

M

Marinated Olives, 105
Mashed Cauliflower, 185
Mixed Berry Frozen Yogurt
  Bar, 200
Moussaka, 174

O

Oatmeal with Berries and
  Sunflower Seeds, 92
One-Pan Tuscan Chicken, 168
Orzo with Spinach and
  Feta, 129

P

Pan-Roasted Salmon with
  Gremolata, 155
Pan-Seared Scallops with
  Sautéed Spinach, 154
Panzanella, 115
Parmesan Zucchini Sticks, 188
Pastaflora, 203
Pasta Puttanesca, 130
Pasta with Pesto, 131
Pizza with Arugula
  and Balsamic
  Glaze, 134–135

Pizza with Red Bell Peppers,
    Basil, Arugula, and
    Caramelized Onion, 136
Poached Eggs with Avocado
    Purée, 97
Pollock with Roasted
    Tomatoes, 161

R
Red Wine Poached Pears, 198
Rice and Spinach, 125
Roasted Asparagus with
    Lemon and Pine
    Nuts, 183
Roasted Fennel with
    Tomatoes, 190
Rosemary Baked Chicken
    Drumsticks, 171

S
Salmon Burgers, 156
Shrimp Mojo de Ajo, 153
Shrimp Scampi, 152
Simple Summer
    Gazpacho, 116
Smoked Salmon Scramble, 96

Spaghetti Squash
    Marinara, 145
Spanakopita, 148–149
Spiced Almonds, 102
Spiced Couscous, 126
Spinach and Feta–Stuffed
    Chicken Breasts, 170
Steak with Red Wine–
    Mushroom
    Sauce, 176–177
Stuffed Red Bell Peppers, 140
Sun-Dried Tomato
    and Artichoke
    Pizza, 132–133
Sweet-and-Savory
    Popcorn, 103
Sweet Potato Mash, 127
Swordfish Kebabs, 158

T
Tabbouleh, 128
Three-Bean Vegetable
    Chili, 144
Tomato and Zucchini
    Frittata, 95
Tourli Greek Baked
    Vegetables, 192

Turkey Burgers with Mango
    Salsa, 164
Tzatziki Sauce, 106

V
Vanilla Pudding with
    Strawberries, 199

W
White Bean Dip, 104
White Bean Soup with
    Kale, 118

Y
Yogurt with Blueberries,
    Honey, and Mint, 90

Z
Zucchini and Meatball
    Soup, 121
Zucchini Noodles with Peas
    and Mint, 146

Index

A

Aerobic exercise, 28, 30–31
Almond milk
  Almond and Maple Quick
    Grits, 91
  Carrot and Bran Mini
    Muffins, 93
  Chocolate Banana
    Smoothie, 87
  French Toast, 94
  Fruit Smoothie, 88
  Oatmeal with Berries and
    Sunflower Seeds, 92
  Sweet Potato Mash, 127
  Tomato and Zucchini
    Frittata, 95
  Yogurt with Blueberries,
    Honey, and Mint, 91
Almonds
  Almond and Maple Quick
    Grits, 91
  Date Nut Energy Balls, 202
  Lemon Kale with Slivered
    Almonds, 189
  Spiced Almonds, 102
*American Journal of Clinical
  Nutrition*, 13
Annals of Family Medicine, 37
Apples
  Baked Apples with Walnuts
    and Spices, 197
  Julene's Green Juice, 86
Apricots, dried
  Easy Trail Mix, 107
  Spiced Couscous, 126
Artichoke hearts
  Artichokes Aginares al
    Greco, 193
  Chop Chop Salad, 114
  Farro with Artichoke
    Hearts, 124

Sun-Dried Tomato
  and Artichoke
  Pizza, 132–133
Asiago cheese
  Pizza with Red Bell
    Peppers, Basil, Arugula,
    and Caramelized
    Onion, 136
  Sun-Dried Tomato
    and Artichoke
    Pizza, 132–133
Asparagus
  Roasted Asparagus with
    Lemon and Pine
    Nuts, 183
Avocados
  Poached Eggs with Avocado
    Purée, 97

B

Balanced plate, 22
Bananas
  Chocolate Banana
    Smoothie, 87
Basal metabolic rate (BMR), 13
Basil
  Baked Stuffed Portobello
    Mushrooms, 141
  Caprese Salad, 112
  Chop Chop Salad, 114
  Cioppino, 159
  Flatbread with Olive
    Tapenade, 137
  One-Pan Tuscan
    Chicken, 168
  Panzanella, 115
  Pasta Puttanesca, 130
  Pasta with Pesto, 131

Pizza with Red Bell
  Peppers, Basil, Arugula,
  and Caramelized
  Onion, 136
Poached Eggs with Avocado
  Purée, 97
Simple Summer
  Gazpacho, 116
Zucchini and Meatball
  Soup, 121
Beans and legumes.
  See also Chickpeas
  Baked Gigante Beans, 143
  Lamb with String
    Beans, 179
  Lentil Soup, 119
  One-Pan Tuscan
    Chicken, 168
  Three-Bean Vegetable
    Chili, 144
  Tourli Greek Baked
    Vegetables, 192
  White Bean Dip, 104
  White Bean Soup with
    Kale, 118
Beef
  Steak with Red
    Wine–Mushroom
    Sauce, 176–177
Bell peppers. *See also* Roasted
  red peppers
  Baked Stuffed Portobello
    Mushrooms, 141
  Chicken and Vegetable
    Soup, 120
  Chicken Sausage and
    Peppers, 166
  Moussaka, 174
  One-Pan Tuscan
    Chicken, 168

Pizza with Red Bell
    Peppers, Basil, Arugula,
    and Caramelized
    Onion, 136
Simple Summer
    Gazpacho, 116
Stuffed Red Bell
    Peppers, 140
Swordfish Kebabs, 158
Three-Bean Vegetable
    Chili, 144
Tourli Greek Baked
    Vegetables, 192
White Bean Soup with
    Kale, 118
Berries. *See specific*
Blackberries
Berry and Yogurt
    Parfait, 89
Mixed Berry Frozen Yogurt
    Bar, 200
Blueberries
Fruit Salad with Yogurt
    Cream, 201
Fruit Smoothie, 88
Mixed Berry Frozen Yogurt
    Bar, 200
Oatmeal with Berries and
    Sunflower Seeds, 92
Yogurt with Blueberries,
    Honey, and Mint, 90
Body mass index (BMI), 13
Broccoli
Broccoli with Ginger and
    Garlic, 186
Brussels sprouts
Easy Brussels Sprouts
    Hash, 182

C

Calories
the balanced plate, 22
caloric intake, 12
and portion control, 18–20
protein, 13
Cantaloupe
Fruit Salad with Yogurt
    Cream, 201

Capers
Chicken Piccata, 167
Flatbread with Olive
    Tapenade, 137
Halibut en Papillote with
    Capers, Onions, Olives,
    and Tomatoes, 160
Panzanella, 115
Pasta Puttanesca, 130
Salmon Burgers, 156
Smoked Salmon
    Scramble, 96
Carbohydrates, caloric
    intake, 14
Cardio exercises, 28, 30–31
Carrots
Artichokes Aginares al
    Greco, 193
Baked Gigante Beans, 143
Balsamic Roasted
    Carrots, 187
Butternut Squash
    Soup, 117
Carrot and Bran Mini
    Muffins, 93
Chicken and Vegetable
    Soup, 120
Chicken with Potatoes,
    Figs, and Carrots, 172
Lentil Soup, 119
Tourli Greek Baked
    Vegetables, 192
White Bean Soup with
    Kale, 118
Cashews
Easy Trail Mix, 107
Cauliflower
Mashed Cauliflower, 185
Celery
Artichokes Aginares al
    Greco, 193
Butternut Squash
    Soup, 117
Lentil Soup, 119
Centers for Disease Control
    and Prevention (CDC),
    17, 28, 37
Cheese. *See specific*

Chicken
Chicken and Vegetable
    Soup, 120
Chicken with Potatoes,
    Figs, and Carrots, 172
Chicken Gyros with
    Tzatziki, 173
Chicken Kapama, 169
Chicken Piccata, 167
Chicken Sausage and
    Peppers, 166
Chop Chop Salad, 114
One-Pan Tuscan
    Chicken, 168
Rosemary Baked Chicken
    Drumsticks, 171
Spinach and Feta–Stuffed
    Chicken Breasts, 170
White Bean Soup with
    Kale, 118
Chickpeas
Chickpea Salad, 113
Falafel Patties, 142
Hummus, 100
Chives
Chop Chop Salad, 114
Chocolate. *See* Cocoa powder
Cilantro
Falafel Patties, 142
Shrimp Mojo de Ajo, 153
Turkey Burgers with Mango
    Salsa, 164
Cocoa powder
Chocolate Banana
    Smoothie, 87
Date Nut Energy Balls, 202
Coconut
Date Nut Energy Balls, 202
Crabmeat
Crab Cakes with Shaved
    Fennel Salad, 157
Cranberries, dried
Easy Trail Mix, 107
Spiced Couscous, 126
Cravings, 73
Cucumbers
Chickpea Salad, 113
Cucumber Salad, 111
Greek Salad, 110

Julene's Green Juice, 86
Panzanella, 115
Tabbouleh, 128
Tzatziki Sauce, 106

D

Dairy-free
  Almond and Maple Quick
    Grits, 91
  Artichokes Aginares al
    Greco, 193
  Baba Ganoush, 101
  Baked Apples with Walnuts
    and Spices, 197
  Baked Gigante Beans, 143
  Balsamic Roasted
    Carrots, 187
  Broccoli with Ginger and
    Garlic, 186
  Butternut Squash
    Soup, 117
  Carrot and Bran Mini
    Muffins, 93
  Chicken and Vegetable
    Soup, 120
  Chicken with Potatoes,
    Figs, and Carrots, 172
  Chicken Kapama, 169
  Chicken Piccata, 167
  Chicken Sausage and
    Peppers, 166
  Chickpea Salad, 113
  Chocolate Banana
    Smoothie, 87
  Cioppino, 159
  Citrus Sautéed
    Spinach, 184
  Cucumber Salad, 111
  Dijon and Herb Pork
    Tenderloin, 175
  Easy Brussels Sprouts
    Hash, 182
  Easy Trail Mix, 107
  Falafel Patties, 142
  Flatbread with Olive
    Tapenade, 137

French Toast, 94
Fruit Smoothie, 88
Greek Meatballs, 178
Halibut en Papillote with
  Capers, Onions, Olives,
  and Tomatoes, 160
Herb-Roasted Turkey
  Breast, 165
Hummus, 100
Julene's Green Juice, 86
Lamb with String
  Beans, 179
Lemon and Watermelon
  Granita, 196
Lentil Soup, 119
Marinated Olives, 105
Oatmeal with Berries and
  Sunflower Seeds, 92
One-Pan Tuscan
  Chicken, 168
Pan-Roasted Salmon with
  Gremolata, 155
Pan-Seared Scallops with
  Sautéed Spinach, 154
Panzanella, 115
Pasta Puttanesca, 130
Pizza with Arugula
  and Balsamic
  Glaze, 134–135
Poached Eggs with Avocado
  Purée, 97
Red Wine Poached
  Pears, 198
Rice and Spinach, 125
Roasted Asparagus with
  Lemon and Pine
  Nuts, 183
Roasted Fennel with
  Tomatoes, 190
Rosemary Baked Chicken
  Drumsticks, 171
Shrimp Mojo de Ajo, 153
Shrimp Scampi, 152
Simple Summer
  Gazpacho, 116
Smoked Salmon
  Scramble, 96
Spaghetti Squash
  Marinara, 145

Spiced Almonds, 102
Spiced Couscous, 126
Steak with Red
  Wine–Mushroom
  Sauce, 176–177
Sweet-and-Savory
  Popcorn, 103
Swordfish Kebabs, 158
Tabbouleh, 128
Three-Bean Vegetable
  Chili, 144
Tourli Greek Baked
  Vegetables, 192
Turkey Burgers with Mango
  Salsa, 164
White Bean Dip, 104
White Bean Soup with
  Kale, 118
Zucchini and Meatball
  Soup, 121
Zucchini Noodles with Peas
  and Mint, 146
Dates
  Date Nut Energy Balls, 202
Dieting. *See* Mediterranean
  diet; Weight loss
Dill
  Artichokes Aginares al
    Greco, 193
  Baked Gigante Beans, 143
  Cucumber Salad, 111
  Salmon Burgers, 156
  Spanakopita, 148–149
  Tzatziki Sauce, 106

E

"Eating the rainbow," 15
Eggplant
  Baba Ganoush, 101
  Moussaka, 174
  Tourli Greek Baked
    Vegetables, 192
Eggs
  Carrot and Bran Mini
    Muffins, 93
  French Toast, 94
  Greek Meatballs, 178
  Moussaka, 174

Pastaflora, 203
Poached Eggs with Avocado
    Purée, 97
Salmon Burgers, 156
Smoked Salmon
    Scramble, 96
Spanakopita, 148–149
Tomato and Zucchini
    Frittata, 95
Vanilla Pudding with
    Strawberries, 199
yolk uses, 95
Exercise
    about, 17, 28
    myths, 30
    planning worksheets, 50,
        56, 62, 68
    recommendation table, 31
    routine setting, 30–31
    strength training, 31–36
    workout tips, 29, 73

F
Fats and oils
    about, 5
    caloric intake, 14
Fennel
    Chicken and Vegetable
        Soup, 120
    Cioppino, 159
    Crab Cakes with Shaved
        Fennel Salad, 157
    Roasted Fennel with
        Tomatoes, 190
Feta cheese
    Greek Salad, 110
    Orzo with Spinach and
        Feta, 129
    Spanakopita, 148–149
    Spinach and Feta–Stuffed
        Chicken Breasts, 170
    Stuffed Red Bell
        Peppers, 140
Figs
    Chicken with Potatoes,
        Figs, and Carrots, 172

Fish. *See also* Salmon
    Cioppino, 159
    Halibut en Papillote with
        Capers, Onions, Olives,
        and Tomatoes, 160
    Pollock with Roasted
        Tomatoes, 161
    Swordfish Kebabs, 158
Fruits. *See specific*

G
Garlic
    Broccoli with Ginger and
        Garlic, 186
    cooking, 186
    Shrimp Mojo de Ajo, 153
    Shrimp Scampi, 152
Ginger
    Broccoli with Ginger and
        Garlic, 186
    Julene's Green Juice, 86
    Red Wine Poached
        Pears, 198
Gluten-free
    Almond and Maple Quick
        Grits, 91
    Artichokes Aginares al
        Greco, 193
    Baba Ganoush, 101
    Baked Apples with Walnuts
        and Spices, 197
    Baked Gigante Beans, 143
    Baked Stuffed Portobello
        Mushrooms, 141
    Balsamic Roasted
        Carrots, 187
    Berry and Yogurt
        Parfait, 89
    Broccoli with Ginger and
        Garlic, 186
    Butternut Squash
        Soup, 117
    Caprese Salad, 112
    Chicken and Vegetable
        Soup, 120
    Chicken with Potatoes,
        Figs, and Carrots, 172
    Chicken Gyros with
        Tzatziki, 173

Chicken Kapama, 169
Chicken Sausage and
    Peppers, 166
Chickpea Salad, 113
Chocolate Banana
    Smoothie, 87
Chop Chop Salad, 114
Cioppino, 159
Citrus Sautéed
    Spinach, 184
Crab Cakes with Shaved
    Fennel Salad, 157
Cucumber Salad, 111
Date Nut Energy Balls, 202
Dijon and Herb Pork
    Tenderloin, 175
Easy Brussels Sprouts
    Hash, 182
Easy Trail Mix, 107
Easy Zucchini Lasagna
    Wraps, 147
Falafel Patties, 142
Fruit Salad with Yogurt
    Cream, 201
Fruit Smoothie, 88
Greek Salad, 110
Grilled Zucchini
    with Yogurt and
    Pomegranate, 191
Halibut en Papillote with
    Capers, Onions, Olives,
    and Tomatoes, 160
Herb-Roasted Turkey
    Breast, 165
Hummus, 100
Julene's Green Juice, 86
Lamb with String
    Beans, 179
Lemon and Watermelon
    Granita, 196
Lemon Kale with Slivered
    Almonds, 189
Lentil Soup, 119
Marinated Olives, 105
Mashed Cauliflower, 185
Mixed Berry Frozen Yogurt
    Bar, 200
Oatmeal with Berries and
    Sunflower Seeds, 92

One-Pan Tuscan
    Chicken, 168
Pan-Roasted Salmon with
    Gremolata, 155
Pan-Seared Scallops with
    Sautéed Spinach, 154
Parmesan Zucchini
    Sticks, 188
Poached Eggs with Avocado
    Purée, 97
Red Wine Poached
    Pears, 198
Rice and Spinach, 125
Roasted Asparagus with
    Lemon and Pine
    Nuts, 183
Roasted Fennel with
    Tomatoes, 190
Rosemary Baked Chicken
    Drumsticks, 171
Shrimp Mojo de Ajo, 153
Simple Summer
    Gazpacho, 116
Smoked Salmon
    Scramble, 96
Spaghetti Squash
    Marinara, 145
Spiced Almonds, 102
Spinach and Feta–Stuffed
    Chicken Breasts, 170
Stuffed Red Bell
    Peppers, 140
Sweet-and-Savory
    Popcorn, 103
Sweet Potato Mash, 127
Swordfish Kebabs, 158
Three-Bean Vegetable
    Chili, 144
Tomato and Zucchini
    Frittata, 95
Tourli Greek Baked
    Vegetables, 192
Turkey Burgers with Mango
    Salsa, 164
Tzatziki Sauce, 106
Vanilla Pudding with
    Strawberries, 199
White Bean Dip, 104

White Bean Soup with
    Kale, 118
Yogurt with Blueberries,
    Honey, and Mint, 90, 91
Zucchini and Meatball
    Soup, 121
Zucchini Noodles with Peas
    and Mint, 146
Goal-setting, 23–25
Grains. *See also* Oats; Rice
    about, 6
    Carrot and Bran Mini
        Muffins, 93
    Farro with Artichoke
        Hearts, 124
    Spiced Couscous, 126
    Tabbouleh, 128
Grapes
    Fruit Salad with Yogurt
        Cream, 201
Greek yogurt
    Berry and Yogurt
        Parfait, 89
    Chop Chop Salad, 114
    Fruit Salad with Yogurt
        Cream, 201
    Grilled Zucchini
        with Yogurt and
        Pomegranate, 191
    Moussaka, 174
    Salmon Burgers, 156
    Tzatziki Sauce, 106
    Yogurt with Blueberries,
        Honey, and Mint, 90
Grits
    Almond and Maple Quick
        Grits, 91

H

Habits
    about, 21
    tracking worksheets, 50,
        56, 62, 68
Harvard School of Public
    Health, 14
Hazelnuts
    Easy Trail Mix, 107
Healthy fats. *See* Fats and oils
Herbs, fresh. *See specific*

Honey
    Baked Apples with Walnuts
        and Spices, 197
    Carrot and Bran Mini
        Muffins, 93
    Chocolate Banana
        Smoothie, 87
    Fruit Salad with Yogurt
        Cream, 201
    Lemon and Watermelon
        Granita, 196
    Pizza with Arugula
        and Balsamic
        Glaze, 134–135
    Red Wine Poached
        Pears, 198
    Yogurt with Blueberries,
        Honey, and Mint, 90
Hydration, 37

J

Jalapeño peppers
    Turkey Burgers with Mango
        Salsa, 164
*Journal of Clinical
    Endocrinology and
    Metabolism*, 38

K

Kale
    Baked Stuffed Portobello
        Mushrooms, 141
    Lemon Kale with Slivered
        Almonds, 189
    White Bean Soup with
        Kale, 118

L

Lamb
    Lamb with String
        Beans, 179
Leafy greens. *See also*
    Kale; Spinach
    Chop Chop Salad, 114
    Greek Salad, 110
    Julene's Green Juice, 86

Pizza with Arugula
and Balsamic
Glaze, 134–135
Pizza with Red Bell
Peppers, Basil, Arugula,
and Caramelized
Onion, 136
Lemons and lemon juice
Artichokes Aginares al
Greco, 193
Baba Ganoush, 101
Chicken Piccata, 167
Chickpea Salad, 113
Chop Chop Salad, 114
Crab Cakes with Shaved
Fennel Salad, 157
Falafel Patties, 142
Farro with Artichoke
Hearts, 124
Greek Salad, 110
Herb-Roasted Turkey
Breast, 165
Hummus, 100
Julene's Green Juice, 86
Lemon and Watermelon
Granita, 196
Lemon Kale with Slivered
Almonds, 189
Marinated Olives, 105
Orzo with Spinach and
Feta, 129
Pan-Roasted Salmon with
Gremolata, 155
Poached Eggs with Avocado
Purée, 97
Roasted Asparagus with
Lemon and Pine
Nuts, 183
Rosemary Baked Chicken
Drumsticks, 171
Salmon Burgers, 156
Shrimp Scampi, 152
Spinach and Feta–Stuffed
Chicken Breasts, 170
Tabbouleh, 128
Tourli Greek Baked
Vegetables, 192
Zucchini Noodles with Peas
and Mint, 146

Leptin, 17
Limes and lime juice
Shrimp Mojo de Ajo, 153
Turkey Burgers with Mango
Salsa, 164

M
Mangos
Turkey Burgers with Mango
Salsa, 164
Maple syrup
Almond and Maple Quick
Grits, 91
Meal in one
Artichokes Aginares al
Greco, 193
Baked Stuffed Portobello
Mushrooms, 141
Berry and Yogurt
Parfait, 89
Chicken and Vegetable
Soup, 120
Chicken with Potatoes,
Figs, and Carrots, 172
Chicken Kapama, 169
Chocolate Banana
Smoothie, 87
Chop Chop Salad, 114
Cioppino, 159
Crab Cakes with Shaved
Fennel Salad, 157
Flatbread with Olive
Tapenade, 137
Fruit Smoothie, 88
Greek Salad, 110
Halibut en Papillote with
Capers, Onions, Olives,
and Tomatoes, 160
Lamb with String
Beans, 179
Moussaka, 174
Oatmeal with Berries and
Sunflower Seeds, 92
One-Pan Tuscan
Chicken, 168
Pan-Seared Scallops with
Sautéed Spinach, 154

Pasta Puttanesca, 130
Pasta with Pesto, 131
Pizza with Arugula
and Balsamic
Glaze, 134–135
Pizza with Red Bell
Peppers, Basil, Arugula,
and Caramelized
Onion, 136
Poached Eggs with Avocado
Purée, 97
Pollock with Roasted
Tomatoes, 161
Shrimp Mojo de Ajo, 153
Shrimp Scampi, 152
Smoked Salmon
Scramble, 96
Spaghetti Squash
Marinara, 145
Stuffed Red Bell
Peppers, 140
Sun-Dried Tomato
and Artichoke
Pizza, 132–133
Three-Bean Vegetable
Chili, 144
Tomato and Zucchini
Frittata, 95
White Bean Soup with
Kale, 118
Yogurt with Blueberries,
Honey, and Mint, 90
Zucchini and Meatball
Soup, 121
Zucchini Noodles with Peas
and Mint, 146
Meal planning
supplemental week
1, 76–77
supplemental week
2, 78–79
week 1, 45–49
week 2, 51–55
week 3, 57–61
week 4, 63–67
worksheet, 80–81
Mediterranean diet
about, 6, 8
and caloric intake, 12–14

exercise and, 17, 28
food pyramid, 7
and lifestyle, 6, 8
menu plan
    worksheet, 80–81
nutrition, 15
supplemental menu
    plans, 76–79
28-day plan, 43–69
and weight loss, 5
Milk. *See also* Almond milk
Chocolate Banana
    Smoothie, 87
Mashed Cauliflower, 185
Vanilla Pudding with
    Strawberries, 199
Mindfulness, 16, 18
Mint
Greek Meatballs, 178
Tabbouleh, 128
Yogurt with Blueberries,
    Honey, and Mint, 90
Zucchini Noodles with Peas
    and Mint, 146
Mozzarella cheese
Baked Stuffed Portobello
    Mushrooms, 141
Caprese Salad, 112
Chop Chop Salad, 114
Easy Zucchini Lasagna
    Wraps, 147
Pizza with Red Bell
    Peppers, Basil, Arugula,
    and Caramelized
    Onion, 136
Mushrooms
Baked Stuffed Portobello
    Mushrooms, 141
Shrimp Mojo de Ajo, 153
Steak with Red
    Wine–Mushroom
    Sauce, 176–177

N
Nutrition, 15
Nuts and seeds, 6. *See also*
    specific

O
Oats
Carrot and Bran Mini
    Muffins, 93
Oatmeal with Berries and
    Sunflower Seeds, 92
Olives
Flatbread with Olive
    Tapenade, 137
Greek Salad, 110
Halibut en Papillote with
    Capers, Onions, Olives,
    and Tomatoes, 160
Marinated Olives, 105
Orzo with Spinach and
    Feta, 129
Pasta Puttanesca, 130
Onions
Baked Gigante Beans, 143
Halibut en Papillote with
    Capers, Onions, Olives,
    and Tomatoes, 160
Lentil Soup, 119
Pizza with Red Bell
    Peppers, Basil, Arugula,
    and Caramelized
    Onion, 136
Tourli Greek Baked
    Vegetables, 192
Oranges and orange juice
Citrus Sautéed
    Spinach, 184
French Toast, 94
Julene's Green Juice, 86
Pan-Seared Scallops with
    Sautéed Spinach, 154
Pastaflora, 203
Red Wine Poached
    Pears, 198
Rice and Spinach, 125
Spiced Couscous, 126
Swordfish Kebabs, 158
White Bean Dip, 104
Oregano
Flatbread with Olive
    Tapenade, 137
Greek Salad, 110
Greek Meatballs, 178

P
Parmesan cheese
Farro with Artichoke
    Hearts, 124
Mashed Cauliflower, 185
Moussaka, 174
Parmesan Zucchini
    Sticks, 188
Pasta with Pesto, 131
Tomato and Zucchini
    Frittata, 95
Parsley
Baba Ganoush, 101
Chicken with Potatoes,
    Figs, and Carrots, 172
Chicken Piccata, 167
Dijon and Herb Pork
    Tenderloin, 175
Falafel Patties, 142
Greek Meatballs, 178
Herb-Roasted Turkey
    Breast, 165
Hummus, 100
Julene's Green Juice, 86
Moussaka, 174
Pan-Roasted Salmon with
    Gremolata, 155
Pollock with Roasted
    Tomatoes, 161
Salmon Burgers, 156
Shrimp Scampi, 152
Tabbouleh, 128
Tourli Greek Baked
    Vegetables, 192
Pasta
Orzo with Spinach and
    Feta, 129
Pasta Puttanesca, 130
Pasta with Pesto, 131
Shrimp Scampi, 152
Peaches
Fruit Salad with Yogurt
    Cream, 201
Pears
Red Wine Poached
    Pears, 198

Peas
    Artichokes Aginares al
        Greco, 193
    Zucchini Noodles with Peas
        and Mint, 146
Pineapple
    Julene's Green Juice, 86
Pine nuts
    Pasta with Pesto, 131
    Roasted Asparagus with
        Lemon and Pine
        Nuts, 183
Plums
    Fruit Salad with Yogurt
        Cream, 201
Pomegranate seeds
    Grilled Zucchini
        with Yogurt and
        Pomegranate, 191
Pork
    Dijon and Herb Pork
        Tenderloin, 175
Portion control, 18–20
Potatoes. *See also* Sweet
    potatoes
    Chicken with Potatoes,
        Figs, and Carrots, 172
    Tourli Greek Baked
        Vegetables, 192
Process goals, 23
Proteins, caloric intake, 13
Puréeing hot liquids, 117

R
Raisins
    Carrot and Bran Mini
        Muffins, 93
Raspberries
    Berry and Yogurt
        Parfait, 89
    Mixed Berry Frozen Yogurt
        Bar, 200
    Oatmeal with Berries and
        Sunflower Seeds, 92
Rest and relaxation,
    17, 37–39
Rice
    Rice and Spinach, 125
    Shrimp Mojo de Ajo, 153

Stuffed Red Bell
    Peppers, 140
Ricotta cheese
    Easy Zucchini Lasagna
        Wraps, 147
Roasted red peppers
    Flatbread with Olive
        Tapenade, 137
Rosemary
    Dijon and Herb Pork
        Tenderloin, 175
    Farro with Artichoke
        Hearts, 124
    Herb-Roasted Turkey
        Breast, 165
    Marinated Olives, 105
    Rosemary Baked Chicken
        Drumsticks, 171

S
Salmon
    Cioppino, 159
    Pan-Roasted Salmon with
        Gremolata, 155
    Salmon Burgers, 156
    Smoked Salmon
        Scramble, 96
Scallions
    Crab Cakes with Shaved
        Fennel Salad, 157
    Cucumber Salad, 111
    Orzo with Spinach and
        Feta, 129
    Salmon Burgers, 156
    Tabbouleh, 128
Scallops
    Pan-Seared Scallops with
        Sautéed Spinach, 154
Self-doubt, 16
Serving sizes, 20
Shallots
    Pollock with Roasted
        Tomatoes, 161
    Shrimp Scampi, 152
    Zucchini Noodles with Peas
        and Mint, 146
Shrimp
    Cioppino, 159

Crab Cakes with Shaved
    Fennel Salad, 157
    Shrimp Mojo de Ajo, 153
    Shrimp Scampi, 152
Sleep, 17, 37–39
SMART goals, 23, 25
Snacks, 44
Spinach
    Citrus Sautéed
        Spinach, 184
    Orzo with Spinach and
        Feta, 129
    Pan-Seared Scallops with
        Sautéed Spinach, 154
    Rice and Spinach, 125
    Spanakopita, 148–149
    Spinach and Feta–Stuffed
        Chicken Breasts, 170
    Stuffed Red Bell
        Peppers, 140
Spiralizing, 146
Squash. *See also* Zucchini
    Butternut Squash
        Soup, 117
    Spaghetti Squash
        Marinara, 145
    Tourli Greek Baked
        Vegetables, 192
Standard American diet, 4–5
Strawberries
    Mixed Berry Frozen Yogurt
        Bar, 200
    Vanilla Pudding with
        Strawberries, 199
Strength training
    core exercises, 33
    full body exercises, 36
    lower body
        exercises, 35–36
    sample routines, 31–32
    upper body
        exercises, 34–35
Stress, 4
Sunflower seeds
    Baba Ganoush, 101
    Oatmeal with Berries and
        Sunflower Seeds, 92
Sweet potatoes
    Sweet Potato Mash, 127

T

Tahini
  Baba Ganoush, 101
  Chickpea Salad, 113
  Hummus, 100
Thyme
  Dijon and Herb Pork
    Tenderloin, 175
  Farro with Artichoke
    Hearts, 124
  Halibut en Papillote with
    Capers, Onions, Olives,
    and Tomatoes, 160
  Herb-Roasted Turkey
    Breast, 165
  Marinated Olives, 105
  White Bean Dip, 104
Tomatoes
  Baked Gigante Beans, 143
  Caprese Salad, 112
  Chicken and Vegetable
    Soup, 120
  Chicken Kapama, 169
  Chop Chop Salad, 114
  Cucumber Salad, 111
  Easy Zucchini Lasagna
    Wraps, 147
  Falafel Patties, 142
  Greek Salad, 110
  Halibut en Papillote with
    Capers, Onions, Olives,
    and Tomatoes, 160
  Lamb with String
    Beans, 179
  Moussaka, 174
  One-Pan Tuscan
    Chicken, 168
  Panzanella, 115
  Pasta Puttanesca, 130
  Pollock with Roasted
    Tomatoes, 161
  Roasted Fennel with
    Tomatoes, 190
  Simple Summer
    Gazpacho, 116
  Spaghetti Squash
    Marinara, 145

  Stuffed Red Bell
    Peppers, 140
  Sun-Dried Tomato
    and Artichoke
    Pizza, 132–133
  Tabbouleh, 128
  Three-Bean Vegetable
    Chili, 144
  Tomato and Zucchini
    Frittata, 95
  Tourli Greek Baked
    Vegetables, 192
  Zucchini and Meatball
    Soup, 121
Turkey
  Greek Meatballs, 178
  Herb-Roasted Turkey
    Breast, 165
  Moussaka, 174
  Turkey Burgers with Mango
    Salsa, 164
  Zucchini and Meatball
    Soup, 121

U

Under 30 minutes
  Almond and Maple Quick
    Grits, 91
  Berry and Yogurt
    Parfait, 89
  Broccoli with Ginger and
    Garlic, 186
  Caprese Salad, 112
  Carrot and Bran Mini
    Muffins, 93
  Chicken and Vegetable
    Soup, 120
  Chicken Piccata, 167
  Chicken Sausage and
    Peppers, 166
  Chickpea Salad, 113
  Chocolate Banana
    Smoothie, 87
  Chop Chop Salad, 114
  Cioppino, 159
  Citrus Sautéed
    Spinach, 184

  Crab Cakes with Shaved
    Fennel Salad, 157
  Cucumber Salad, 111
  Date Nut Energy Balls, 202
  Easy Brussels Sprouts
    Hash, 182
  Easy Trail Mix, 107
  French Toast, 94
  Fruit Salad with Yogurt
    Cream, 201
  Fruit Smoothie, 88
  Greek Salad, 110
  Grilled Zucchini
    with Yogurt and
    Pomegranate, 191
  Halibut en Papillote with
    Capers, Onions, Olives,
    and Tomatoes, 160
  Hummus, 100
  Julene's Green Juice, 86
  Lemon Kale with Slivered
    Almonds, 189
  Lentil Soup, 119
  Mashed Cauliflower, 185
  Mixed Berry Frozen Yogurt
    Bar, 200
  Oatmeal with Berries and
    Sunflower Seeds, 92
  Orzo with Spinach and
    Feta, 129
  Pan-Roasted Salmon with
    Gremolata, 155
  Pan-Seared Scallops with
    Sautéed Spinach, 154
  Panzanella, 115
  Parmesan Zucchini
    Sticks, 188
  Pasta Puttanesca, 130
  Pasta with Pesto, 131
  Poached Eggs with Avocado
    Purée, 97
  Rice and Spinach, 125
  Roasted Asparagus with
    Lemon and Pine
    Nuts, 183
  Salmon Burgers, 156
  Shrimp Scampi, 152

Smoked Salmon
Scramble, 96
Spiced Almonds, 102
Spiced Couscous, 126
Sweet-and-Savory
Popcorn, 103
Sweet Potato Mash, 127
Swordfish Kebabs, 158
Tabbouleh, 128
Tomato and Zucchini
Frittata, 95
Turkey Burgers with Mango
Salsa, 164
White Bean Dip, 104
Yogurt with Blueberries,
Honey, and Mint, 90
Zucchini Noodles with Peas
and Mint, 146

V
Vegan
Almond and Maple Quick
Grits, 91
Artichokes Aginares al
Greco, 193
Baba Ganoush, 101
Balsamic Roasted
Carrots, 187
Broccoli with Ginger and
Garlic, 186
Butternut Squash
Soup, 117
Chickpea Salad, 113
Citrus Sautéed
Spinach, 184
Cucumber Salad, 111
Date Nut Energy Balls, 202
Easy Trail Mix, 107
Falafel Patties, 142
Farro with Artichoke
Hearts, 124
Fruit Smoothie, 88
Hummus, 100
Julene's Green Juice, 86
Lemon Kale with Slivered
Almonds, 189
Lentil Soup, 119
Marinated Olives, 105

Mashed Cauliflower, 185
Oatmeal with Berries and
Sunflower Seeds, 92
Rice and Spinach, 125
Roasted Asparagus with
Lemon and Pine
Nuts, 183
Roasted Fennel with
Tomatoes, 190
Simple Summer
Gazpacho, 116
Spaghetti Squash
Marinara, 145
Spiced Almonds, 102
Spiced Couscous, 126
Sweet-and-Savory
Popcorn, 103
Sweet Potato Mash, 127
Tabbouleh, 128
Three-Bean Vegetable
Chili, 144
Tourli Greek Baked
Vegetables, 192
White Bean Dip, 104
Zucchini Noodles with Peas
and Mint, 146
Vegetables. See also specific
caloric intake, 14
Vegetarian
Baked Apples with Walnuts
and Spices, 197
Baked Gigante Beans, 143
Baked Stuffed Portobello
Mushrooms, 141
Berry and Yogurt
Parfait, 89
Caprese Salad, 112
Carrot and Bran Mini
Muffins, 93
Chocolate Banana
Smoothie, 87
Easy Brussels Sprouts
Hash, 182
Easy Zucchini Lasagna
Wraps, 147
Flatbread with Olive
Tapenade, 137
French Toast, 94

Fruit Salad with Yogurt
Cream, 201
Greek Salad, 110
Grilled Zucchini
with Yogurt and
Pomegranate, 191
Lemon and Watermelon
Granita, 196
Mixed Berry Frozen Yogurt
Bar, 200
Orzo with Spinach and
Feta, 129
Panzanella, 115
Parmesan Zucchini
Sticks, 188
Pastaflora, 203
Pasta with Pesto, 131
Pizza with Arugula
and Balsamic
Glaze, 134–135
Pizza with Red Bell
Peppers, Basil, Arugula,
and Caramelized
Onion, 136
Poached Eggs with Avocado
Purée, 97
Red Wine Poached
Pears, 198
Spanakopita, 148–149
Stuffed Red Bell
Peppers, 140
Sun-Dried Tomato
and Artichoke
Pizza, 132–133
Tomato and Zucchini
Frittata, 95
Tzatziki Sauce, 106
Vanilla Pudding with
Strawberries, 199
Yogurt with Blueberries,
Honey, and Mint, 90

W
Walnuts
Baked Apples with Walnuts
and Spices, 197
Berry and Yogurt
Parfait, 89

Date Nut Energy Balls, 202
Easy Trail Mix, 107
Mixed Berry Frozen Yogurt
    Bar, 200
Water, 6, 37
Watermelon
    Lemon and Watermelon
        Granita, 196
Weight loss
    the balanced plate, 22
    and calories, 12–14
    goal-setting, 25
    and habits, 21
    holistic approach to, 14–18
    and the
        Mediterranean diet, 5
    portion control, 18–20
    priorities, 72

success tips, 72–75
Workouts. *See* Exercise

Y

Yogurt, frozen. *See also*
    Greek yogurt
Mixed Berry Frozen Yogurt
    Bar, 200

Z

Zesting, 155
Zucchini
    Baked Stuffed Portobello
        Mushrooms, 141
    Chicken and Vegetable
        Soup, 120
    Chop Chop Salad, 114

Easy Zucchini Lasagna
    Wraps, 147
Grilled Zucchini
    with Yogurt and
    Pomegranate, 191
Parmesan Zucchini
    Sticks, 188
Stuffed Red Bell
    Peppers, 140
Tomato and Zucchini
    Frittata, 95
Tourli Greek Baked
    Vegetables, 192
Zucchini and Meatball
    Soup, 121
Zucchini Noodles with Peas
    and Mint, 146

Acknowledgments

To my amazing children, Ella Juliet and Jake Theodore, who inspire me to get up every morning and be the best mom I can. Whose resilience and love have been awe inspiring. Who share me with my work, and fully understand that although they come first, my dedication to my patients is imperative, and I can multitask extremely well. Who know there's "never a day without yogurt," and there's always a "kiss" in their lunchbox.

To my yiayia, Julia—my rock, my soulmate, the woman I am named after, who makes everything right. I couldn't be more thrilled to be named after the strongest, most beautiful lady I've ever known. Allowing me to learn in your kitchen and teaching me from such a young age all of your secrets helped spark my love for food and nutrition, and I'm forever grateful.

To my mom, whose food always tasted the best. Who always had a home-cooked meal and lunch for me, and who still delivers my favorites. Your Greek specialties brought our culture to life. Thank you for sharing some of those enduring recipes with me for this book. Both my mom and my dad have always been there to support me; thank you both for that blessing.

To my patients past, present, and future. I love what I do. It is my absolute privilege to be part of your journey to health. Thank you for trusting me and inspiring me every single day.

To the stellar doctors and staff I work with at The Gastroenterology Group of Northern NJ and FL Rehabilitation. You are the best of the best. I'm so proud to work with a team of such brilliant people who are also so kind.

A special thanks to Dr. Mark Sapienza for writing the Foreword. Your expertise and knowledge is so appreciated and significant to this book.

Finally, to you, my readers. I am thrilled that you and I became connected by something so powerful—wellness.

Smiles,

Julene

About the Author

JULENE STASSOU, MS, RD, holds a master's of science degree in nutrition education from Columbia University and is clinically trained in all areas of nutrition.

She has a private practice in northern New Jersey, where she works with children and adults on a wide range of issues, including diet and weight loss and gain, food allergies, digestive issues, eating disorders, cardiovascular health, and diabetes management. Her goal is to help people meet their individual health needs and wellness goals by taking a holistic approach to better health.

Although her primary role is that of a health care provider, in addition to her nutrition expertise, she also brings a culinary background as well as a passion for making a difference in people's lives to her work. She truly loves what she does and is driven by her patients' success.

Julene was named Bergen County's Best Nutritionist in 2015, 2016, and 2017 by *Bergen* magazine. She is a member of the American Dietetic Association. She resides in northern New Jersey where she grew up.

CPSIA information can be obtained
at www.ICGtesting.com
Printed in the USA
JSHW021543300721
17400JS00006B/8